MW01275645

Many Futures of India

Rajiv Kumar is Director General, Federation of Indian Chambers of Commerce and Industry (FICCI), New Delhi. He is the former Director and Chief Executive, ICRIER, one of India's leading economic policy think tanks. He has previously worked with the Government of India, Asian Development Bank (ADB) and Confederation of Indian Industry (CII). He was also member of the National Security Advisory Board. Dr. Kumar is a D.Phil. in Economics from Oxford University and has several publications to his credit. He is also an active columnist.

Many Futures of India

RAJIV KUMAR

ACADEMIC FOUNDATION
NEW DELHI

www.academicfoundation.com

First published in 2011
by

ACADEMIC FOUNDATION
4772-73 / 23 Bharat Ram Road, (23 Ansari Road),
Darya Ganj, New Delhi - 110 002 (India).
Phones : 23245001 / 02 / 03 / 04.
Fax : +91-11-23245005.
E-mail : books@academicfoundation.com
www. academicfoundation.com

Cataloging in Publication Data--DK
  Courtesy: D.K. Agencies (P) Ltd. <docinfo@dkagencies.com>

Kumar, Rajiv, 1951-
  Many futures of India / Rajiv Kumar.
    p.   cm.
  Includes index.
  ISBN 13: 9788171888740
  ISBN 10: 8171888747

  1. Economic development--India. 2. India--Economic policy-
-1991- 3. International economic relations. 4. South Asia--
Economic integration.   I. Title.

DDC 330.954   22

Typeset by Italics India, New Delhi.
Printed and bound in India.

Dedicated to the memory of my father
Shri Vidya Prakash
who taught me the importance of self-esteem

Contents

Section I
The Indian Economy

Section II
Reforms are still needed

Section III
India and the Global Economy

Section IV
India and Global Governance

Section V
South Asia: India's Role

Preface

The volume has been long in the making in as much as the essays contained here were written over the last two years as columns in different newspapers. The essays are therefore in the nature of a commentary on the evolution of the Indian economy over the past few years rather than an attempt at an analytical enquiry in to the state of the Indian economy at any given point of time. This will hopefully provide to the reader with some insights on the on-going India's triple transition which in its scale, complexity and multiplicity of risks and stakes involved makes it a unique experiment in human history. As is argued in the Introduction, an essay specially written for this volume, there has never been another instance of a society as diverse, pluralistic and continental in its demographic and geographic dimensions, attempting to simultaneously transform itself politically, socially and economically. India needs all the luck and even more so the sheer determination of its amazing people to be successful in this audacious undertaking. As the title tries to convey, India's future is still far from certain as significant downside risks still remain and have to be addressed. Hopefully, the readers will find enough material here to be fully warned of the significant dangers of any complacency in handling the on-going transition.

The vibrant intellectual environment at ICRIER, where I was during the time these essays were written, provided the needed stimulus for thinking about the issues and writing the essays. Many colleagues at ICRIER offered not only inputs for these articles but also their comments and criticisms on initial drafts. I wish to acknowledge my gratitude to all of them for these inputs and also for a wonderful four years spent with

them. I sincerely thank the newspapers which gave me the opportunity
to write these columns, particularly the *Financial Chronicle*, where I
contributed a fortnightly column and from where the majority of these
essays are taken. And many thanks to a large number of readers who sent
me their valuable and most appreciated feedback which provided the
needed encouragement to continue with the columns even at times when
it looked virtually impossible given the manifold pressures of managing
a rapidly growing think tank. Sincere thanks to Jennifer of the
International Futures Forum, who agreed to do the illustrations with such
disarming willingness, as if it was simply the most natural thing to do.
Thanks also to Tara and Michelle who went over the manuscript to iron
out the wrinkles in good time. Finally, my heartfelt thanks to Vineeta,
Prashant and Niranand who have never let me feel that my work, which
is really a hobby, has come in the way of enjoying our time together as
a family.

— Rajiv Kumar

1

India's Triple Transition:
A Work in Progress
Introduction

THE first decade of the new century has seen global attention turn to India and thankfully largely for positive reasons. The world seems to have recognised that 'Incredible India', the catchy by-line propagated by the country's Ministry of Tourism, is not just hyperbole but reflects the multifaceted achievements and features of this enigmatic country. The elephant, it seems, can dance after all.

Despite the rather poor initial three years, the Indian economy achieved a creditable GDP growth rate of 7.25 per cent during this decade. The growth rate rises to 8.3 per cent if we take the last seven years, a period which covers the post-Lehman global recession, the worst since the Great Depression. This makes India the second fastest growing economy after China and easily the fastest growing free market economy in the world. India's GDP, which in terms of purchasing power parity (PPP) was $3.5 trillion in 2009, would double every 10 years with an average growth rate of 7.2 per cent and every 9 years at 8 per cent. This implies that the country will emerge as the third largest economy by 2040 with a GDP in PPP terms of more than $28 trillion or more than eight times the current size. At these rates, India's per capita income in 2040 will be almost $20,000 (in PPP terms). These are incredible numbers but indeed probable given the 'power of the exponential' and a policy framework that will allow the economy to grow at its potential rate of growth. Thus, the economy will complete its double transition from a low income to a medium or even a high income economy in the next three decades. In less than a hundred years of independence from nearly two centuries of colonial rule, India will have regained its place amongst the ranks of world's leading economies and emerged as one of the major global powers. This is quite a comment on the country's inherent resilience and the dynamism of its people.

The impressive economic performance briefly described above is itself sufficient reason for India to become the centre of global attention. The more impressive achievement, which has not been generally articulated but must underlie the enormous interest all round the world in India's progress in the last 10 years, is that India's strong economic performance has been a part of the country's rather audacious and historically unprecedented attempt to complete a triple transition in the 60 years since independence. As is evident to any observer of the Indian scene, the country has been simultaneously going through an economic, political and social transition. This is a huge, complex and expectedly a messy undertaking which purports to change in a most fundamental manner the lives and livelihoods of a sixth of humanity. Historically, countries have gone through these transitions in a sequential order, which is expectedly more manageable, less complex and also less costly both in social and economic terms.

The economic transition has seen India changing from a predominantly agrarian economy with agriculture contributing more than 55 per cent of the total GDP in the 1950s, to an economy in which the sector contributed a mere 16 per cent of the total national output in 2009. India's growth paradigm has not followed the standard paradigm with industry and manufacturing taking up the share given up by agriculture. Instead, the services sector, which today accounts for nearly 60 per cent of the output, has shown amazing dynamism and propelled economic growth forward. The share of the manufacturing sector has unfortunately stagnated but is beginning to rise with an increasing number of provincial governments, having recognised the greater employment potential of the industrial sector, actively promoting industrial and manufacturing sector investment in recent years. The economic transition is far from complete

as also the other two transitions. Agriculture remains the predominant sector in terms of employment, absorbing more than half the workforce. The economy is also characterised by a marked dualism with a large share of economic activity and employment happening in the so-called unorganised sector. Productivity and income levels in the unorganised sector of the same industry can be as low as a sixth of those in the organised sector. Working conditions and the regulatory environment can be dramatically different in the two sectors. This is best captured in the oft-made distinction between 'Bharat' and 'India' which coexist but do not necessarily impinge directly on each other. The economic transition must be completed if the country has to achieve its avowed vision of inclusive and rapid growth, which is enshrined in the Indian constitution and has come to be espoused by all political parties across the entire spectrum.

The political transition from a colonised state to a vibrant, strongly competitive and at times a messy democracy has taken a phenomenal amount of resources and good luck. The people, themselves poor and deprived, have borne, sometimes grudgingly, the substantial costs of

building a multiparty parliamentary democracy based on universal franchise in a hugely heterogeneous and diverse society.

This is perhaps an unparalleled achievement especially when we take the massive scale at which this has been done. It could well be that India made a virtue of its necessity. In as pluralistic and diverse, in terms of geography, culture, religion, language and incomes, a society as India, there was and is still no alternative to democracy for establishing a State that has the necessary legitimacy to govern the country, which as several observers have remarked exists more as an idea because of its diversity. There is no single social group that is large enough to be able to exert its dominance over the several 'others' as was sharply demonstrated during the 1960s when there was an attempt to impose Hindi as the national language. Then again the short-lived experience with emergency in the 1970s amply demonstrated that the model of a benevolent oligarchy, so common all over post-colonial Asia, would simply not work in India. In all likelihood, these experiences have prevented even the armed forces, which mirror the national diversity in their composition, from attempting to play a larger and more active role in the country's governance even when the impatient middle classes have persistently demanded it.

In the bargain, however, it became necessary to incur upfront the rather substantive costs of operating a democratic polity and making the political transition. These are in the nature of sunk costs, which as we know, can often be large enough to make the entire enterprise unviable. This could have happened in the case of Indian democracy. And until the emergence of Rajiv Gandhi and his modernising reform agenda, it appeared that the apparent trade-off between a populist democracy and economic growth will become untenable. Only with the onset of reforms in the mid-1980s and their acceleration in the early 1990s, did India learn to handle this important trade-off effectively. And today, the hope is that the country, having incurred the costs, will now be able to derive its 'democratic dividend' with electoral outcomes becoming increasingly dependent not on populist rhetoric but increasingly, though not totally, on the actual performance of the party in power in terms of the delivery of outcomes promised during the electoral campaign. The shift from competitive populism to competitive good governance can be one of the most important bonuses that could accrue in the coming years.

The social transition has entailed the transformation of a highly stratified and feudal society with centuries of tradition and dogma into a modern industrial society that is increasingly integrated with the rest

of the world and shows unmistakable signs of having adopted some cosmopolitan features. Unlike some other countries, India has so far been able to avoid the immense human costs that have historically been associated with such large scale social transitions. The turmoil of costs incurred during partition preceded the ongoing social transition, though of course they have contributed to it. India has tried to achieve its social transition more gradually, sometimes too frustratingly slowly, through a process of education, awareness, legislative initiatives and positive discrimination that has found a prominent place in the country's Constitution. That significant progress, though not sufficient by any means, has taken place and is reflected in a number of ways. We have today a women Dalit (untouchable) chief minister of the most populous state in India. The next most populous state of Bihar has had a chief minister from the intermediate or backward caste for more than two decades. It is a crime to address anybody from the lower and untouchable castes by the caste names that were often in the past used as derogatory terms. The Constitution today guarantees 33 per cent of elected positions in rural local government to women and this is sought to be raised to 50 per cent. In some states, the share of seats in colleges and of open positions in government jobs that are available for being filled by those belonging to upper castes or privileged groups is less than 10 per cent. Many states today have special schemes for supporting the education of the female child and social malpractices like child marriages and dowry have been made illegal, though unfortunately they still continue to blemish the society. I think it will be safe to say that a foreigner living in India today will not be accosted by crude and gross manifestations of social and gender discrimination. Yet it will also be true that those who do stay longer will surely realise that there is still a long road ahead before India emerges as a truly modern, non-discriminatory and merit-based society. Nevertheless, it would be fair to say that fears of caste and religion-based civil strife, that were quite palpable in the years after partition and Independence have now greatly disappeared. India is progressing steadily, with some occasional hiccups and setbacks, towards establishing a more socially equal, secular and modern society.

The triple transitions were initiated immediately after securing independence as these were an integral and important component on the agenda of India's freedom movement. Leaders like Mahatma Gandhi, Jawaharlal Nehru, B.R. Ambedkar and their compatriots had built their reputations and political careers talking about different aspects of the three transitions. However, until the beginning of the 1990s, the overhang of poverty and slothful economic performance ensured that their progress and remarkable nature remained largely unnoticed by the outside world and even by Indians themselves. But this has expectedly changed during the 'noughties' as India has managed rapid economic growth even while, at the same time, going through these multiple transitions. The promising prospect is that if India could successfully handle the threefold transition and, in the process, also manages to eliminate poverty and squalor and give its people a decent level of living by 2047, exactly a 100 years after its independence, it could provide a distinct and workable development paradigm for other developing countries. This would be as epoch making as India's successful experiment of overthrowing colonial rule using primarily non-violent means. Because of its circumstances and because it has the acumen to tailor its development strategy to effectively respond to the ground realities, India, if it is successful in completing the triple transitions, would have demonstrated that diversity, democracy and development can be simultaneously achieved.

But the trillion dollar question surely is whether India will successfully complete its triple transition. There are some in India, and ironically within the leadership across the range of political parties, who believe that this success is already ensured. The glib talk of demographic dividend, India being the flavour of the year in other countries, the world beating Indian entrepreneurs who will simply not take a no for an answer and repeated reference to our glorious past demonstrates this dangerous complacency. The success is far, far from ensured. All three transitions are very much a work in progress and can unfortunately be reversed, if not fully, then in large measure. Examples of this tenuous state of our polity and the economy are far too many to be enumerated here. But some examples may be useful to reinforce the central argument of this volume that any complacency about India's future is dangerous and can be extremely costly.

The economic transition is overshadowed by the continuing backwardness of India's agriculture sector where productivity and income

levels lag far behind the manufacturing and services sector. The marked
dualism in the economy threatens to overwhelm any progress that we
make on the employment front with hardly any jobs being generated in
the organised sector over the last decade. The economic transition could
well be derailed if we cannot absorb the 12 million or so young people
who join the country's workforce each year. With such a massive overhang
of job seekers, it will not be too much complacency to convert the
expected demographic dividend to a demographic nightmare which could
see the country awash in a sea of social discontent and political turbulence
that will stop the economic transition in its tracks.

The political transition faces a rising threat from left wing extremism
and the ever present dangers from religious fundamentalists and ethnic
separatists that have still not seen sufficient merit in hitching their future
to the Indian nation state. These groups, which have so far remained
outside the mainstream, bear no allegiance to the Indian Constitution and
have openly espoused and adopted armed conflict as a justifiable means
for overthrowing the existing order, which is seen as exploitative, repressive
and not responsive to peoples' aspirations. We are told that Naxalism, the
local name for extreme, left wing ideology that has carried several well-
planned armed attacks on Indian security forces, has spread to more than
200 of India's 532 districts. The success of Maoists across the border in
Nepal encourage their counterparts in India in their belief that they can
also come to share or even capture state power by waging a long-drawn,
armed conflict. It is often claimed that the 'glue' that holds this diverse
and disparate country together is strong enough to not permit these
extremist tendencies to become mainstream. This is true so far. But with
rising incidence of domestic insurgencies being actively stoked by outside
powers who may be hoping or even trying for India's balkanisation, either
as revenge or to weaken a potential rival in Asia, can we afford to not
remain perpetually vigilant? Our political transition, will be complete only
when the centripetal forces have gained a strong dominance over
centrifugal tendencies. This requires ongoing efforts to deepen our
democracy, strengthen our political institutions and achieve effective and
accountable governance. The message is surely again that complacency is
completely unwarranted.

With rampant female infanticide, dowry deaths, child marriages, honour killings of young couples daring to break some obscure diktats ordered by *khap* leaders, violence against immigrants from other parts of the country and regular diatribes against other communities by fanatic religious leaders, we can hardly claim that the social transition is complete. In fact, it can easily be argued that the rise of identity politics since the latter half of the 1980s has reversed the gains made during the Independence movement and the first three decades of post-independent development. It is perhaps belabouring the issue to point out that communal and religious symbolism has become more pronounced today than in the past and could attract political patronage, which can make it an explosive mixture. That our social progress can be reversed is perhaps most virulently evident in the ever-increasing pomp and grandeur of religious festivals and the rise of communal forces even in a state like Kerala with its universal literacy and human development indices, which are comparable to advanced economies. Complacency on this count can again be fatal.

India's triple transition, therefore, remains very much a work in progress. And the nature of any ongoing experiment, especially one as complex and at such massive a scale, is that its outcome can hardly be anticipated, let alone be forecast except by those who would like to distract the people from the real tasks at hand. The best we can do is to develop plausible scenarios without assigning probabilities to forewarn ourselves of the many futures that could still unfold for India. Yes, the 21st century can be India's but we will have to strive hard to make it happen and be prepared to break out of our intellectual and existential comfort zones.

The introduction will hopefully provide the necessary context for the 34 articles that are included in this volume. The running theme across these pieces, written as newspaper columns, is that policymakers, industrialists, businessmen, civil society leaders and academics, in short the India's elite, owes it to the common citizens to persist with reforms required to complete the three ongoing transitions. These reforms can neither be imported from any other country as they have to suit the complex Indian reality nor any longer be undertaken by stealth in the face of the hyperactive and inquisitive media that has burgeoned in the last 15 years. A plausible case has to be made and disseminated on how these reforms will improve the lot of the great majority and contribute to inclusive and rapid growth.

The focus of these articles, written principally for business dailies, is necessarily the economic transition. However, having spent one's impressionable youth in arguing that material conditions are the underlying and fundamental basis for all other changes, social or political or cultural, I would tend to argue that these articles deal with some of the most important issues at hand for India. The hope is that these will highlight the importance of undertaking reforms in other equally important areas like the judiciary, political practices and social organisation. The best I can hope for is that these articles when read together, will provide enough food for thought for readers and instigate at least some to carry this discussion forward and intensify the debate. A vigorous and honest debate is a key feature of a vibrant civil society and more importantly it keeps our leaders alert and on their toes. That will to some extent ensure that complacency is avoided.

Section I
The Indian Economy

2

The Many Futures of India

THERE is currently an air of expectation about India's future prospects both within the country and even more so abroad. We are surely on the move. The new century, it is said, will see India emerge as a global player because of its structural advantages. Some of the major ones are, for example, a young population with its promise of an expanding workforce and rising savings; established institutions, which have weathered the vagaries of a boisterous democracy and gathered strength; a dynamic and large entrepreneurial class that simply does not take 'no' for an answer; a vibrant and independent media that is beginning to rediscover its social purpose of enforcing accountability; a traditionally strong value for education; an ability to adapt to changing conditions; and a benevolent geography that so far has shown tremendous resilience against gross misuse but may be giving up now. The danger, however, is that these structural advantages, combined with our predisposition for believing that the future is 'predestined', can generate a dangerous level of complacency and inertia. This fatal flaw could not only lead India to perform below its true potential, but to even move towards chaos, conflict and disaster.

These alternative possibilities for India's future emerge most sharply when we attempt to outline future scenarios as was done by a joint team of the Confederation of Indian Industry (CII) and the World Economic Forum (WEF) in 2006. The team generated three scenarios, and none of us could foresee that outcomes under each of the scenarios for India in

2025 could be so radically different. In the best option called 'Pahle India', the country fulfilled its promise and raced ahead with rapid, inclusive and globally integrated growth to eliminate poverty and emerge as one of the major global powers. The worst scenario called 'Atakta Bharat' had India stumbling along at low growth rates with worsening equity, persistent poverty and growing isolation. 'Atakta Bharat' expectedly also saw increasing social and political stress, resulting in the fragmentation of the country. Having presented the worst scenario on several occasions, I came to realise how eminently possible—though obviously unacceptable—this outcome could be. The principal aim of this piece will be to ask the more difficult and uncomfortable questions to try and provoke us out of our complacency and the easy option of taking our destiny for granted and thereby preventing the worst outcome from being realised.

The scenario-building exercise sharply brought out the critical difference between the best and worst outcomes: the quality of governance and implementation of the next round of reforms. This crucial difference between the two scenarios provides the *raison d'etre* for this piece. Here we will persist in making the case for necessary reforms and their implementation. We will not allow our democracy to become an excuse for political inertia or bureaucratic callousness. This is informed by the belief that reforms in this country—with its thankfully open society, competitive democracy and hyperactive fourth estate—cannot be undertaken by stealth. Reforms have been successfully undertaken only when they were backed by popular opinion and had captured a hegemonic position in people's thinking. This is true of the adoption of the Mahalanobis model, or the switch to capitalist farming under the Green Revolution, or giving a greater role to the public sector after 1969, or the liberalisation of the late 1980s and early 1990s. The truth cannot be further away from the myth that is unfortunately quite widespread: that the 1991 reforms were thrust upon us by the International Monetary Fund (IMF) and the World Bank. The period leading up to July 1991 had seen a range of our top economists, journalists and even civil servants, across a range of political and ideological persuasions, arguing in favour of dismantling the plethora of dysfunctional controls and licences. Reforms followed when the battle of ideas had been decisively won.

Today, we again need a similar discussion and debate on the need for and the nature of the next round of reforms. The absence of such public discourse and pressure is responsible for reform bills continuing to languish in Parliament and the ruling establishment getting away with inaction and even sliding back. This is despite the clear demonstration of the huge benefits that reforms have generated for common people, as in the case of the telecom sector. We need to, therefore, intensify the public discourse on the necessity of such reforms and, in the process, take on some holy cows and bust some well-worn myths. One of them, for example, often heard in industry conclaves and from leaders of large industrial houses, is that India can grow despite its government. We should, perhaps, start by exploding this myth. We need to focus on making the case for reforms that benefit the people and on the need to have these reforms rooted in the Indian reality to be effective.

3

Global Crisis and India's Growth Rate*

INDIA had a dream run of five years during 2003-2008 as the GDP growth averaged nearly 9 per cent annually for five years-the best ever run over five years ever! The economy began to slow down from the middle of 2007-08. A 9 per cent growth apparently could not be sustained, being clearly beyond India's potential rate of growth which has been estimated by more than one agency to be around 8.5 per cent. And as the economy overheated, the central bank tightened credit, slowly initially but harder since 2006-07. As an expected outcome, the economy began to slow down. Some of us had argued that the tightening was going too far and overreacting to inflationary fears, which largely arose from global factors. The policymakers and none of us had foreseen the external shock arising from the global crisis, which began with the financial meltdown in the US. The interesting question therefore is: what would India's growth rate have been in response to the policy measures without the global crisis as compared to what it is likely to be in the context of the ongoing global crisis.

The Indian Council for Research on International Economic Relations (ICRIER) has been forecasting India's GDP growth rate with the use of 'leading indicators'. Leading economic indicators (LEI) are variables that are considered to have a significant influence on the future level of economic activity in the country. These indicators give advance signals

---

* Written in April 2009, some data may now have been revised.

about the likely growth rate and, in this case, we are able to use this to forecast GDP growth five quarters ahead of the value of leading indicators. The predictive quality of LEIs has earned them their name of being 'leading indicators'. It had predicted a growth of GDP at 9.2 per cent for 2007-08 in November 2007, while most agencies had predicted a lower growth rate of 8.5 per cent or below that year as against the actual growth rate of 9 per cent. Then again, ICRIER was first in predicting a growth rate (before the crisis erupted) of 7.8 per cent for 2008-09 in July this year, an estimate that thereafter was adopted by others including both the RBI and the finance minister.

For constructing the leading indicators index, the following 10 indicators have been used: (i) production of machinery and equipment, (ii) sales of heavy commercial vehicles, (iii) non-food credit, (iv) railway freight traffic, (v) cement sales, (vi) sales of the corporate sector, (vii) fuel and metal prices, (viii) real rate of interest, (ix) BSE sensex, and (x) GDP growth rates of the US and Europe.

A composite index for the LEI has been constructed for the period 1997-2008 with the quarterly series of growth of these variables (except for the real rate of interest where the level, and not the growth, has been used) using the 'principal component index' (PCI) method. The PCI method assigns weights to each component leading indicator by the iteration process based on its contribution to total variation in the composite index.

Leading indicators could predict future growth based on what has already happened in the past but cannot capture the impact of sudden external shocks which may have an immediate impact on the economy. Examples of such shocks in the past are the IT boom burst in 2000-01 (Q3: 2000-01 to Q2: 2001-02), crop failure in 2002-03 (Q2 to Q4: 2002-03) and the recent US financial meltdown (starting with Q3: 2008-2009 and say, up to Q2: 2009-10). The LEI index with a 5-quarter lag and the shock represented by a dummy variable (equal to 1 with shock and 0 without) are used to forecast India's future GDP growth. The growth equation builds in the previous shocks of the dotcom bust and the agricultural failure and its estimates track the actual GDP performance very closely as shown in Figure 3.1. For projecting the GDP growth for 2008-09 and the next year, the LEI index incorporates the current expected shock of global financial meltdown.

FIGURE 3.1

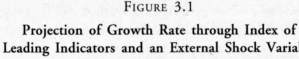

Projection of Growth Rate through Index of
Leading Indicators and an External Shock Variable

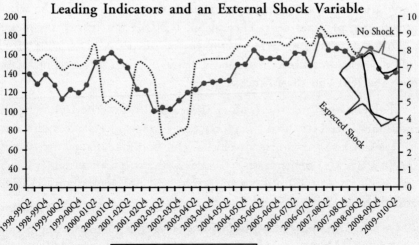

The estimated equation for GDP growth forecast is satisfactory with adjusted R-square value of 0.58 and t-values for the regression co-efficients of 3.24 for LEI (-5) and -5.95 for the shock variable which are significant at 99 per cent level. The GDP forecast for 2008-09 and for the first-half of 2009-10 is tabulated below alternatively for with the shock and without the shock.

TABLE 3.1

GDP Forecast for 2008-09 and H1 2009-10

	No Shock	With Shock
2008-09	7.5	5.8
2009-10 H1	6.8	3.9

As Table 3.1 shows, India would have grown 7.5 per cent this year (a slowdown from 9 per cent in 2007-08), had the global crisis not occurred. The global crisis is likely to bring India's growth rate to below 6 per cent in 2008-09. With the first-half GDP growth rate already known, this implies a sharp slowdown in the next two quarters. In the first-half of next year, the economy would have grown below 7 per cent in the absence of the external crisis. The global crisis may reduce Indian growth rate to as low as less than 4 per cent in 2009-10.[1]

The implications are significant. For starters, the Eleventh Five-Year Plan (2007-2012) targets should be recalibrated immediately if that exercise is to remain credible. We should prepare the people for slowdown in employment generation and plan for countercyclical measures urgently. This should imply an immediate reduction in interest rates to bring down the cost of capital and a quick and thorough review of government procedures that vitiate the investment environment and hike up transactions costs. Rather than throw more money at the problem, it is important to identify infrastructure projects like the highway programme where some additional resources but a lot of attention to implementation and execution can generate additional capacities and help raise growth.

---

1. It may, however, be noted that we have not calibrated the intensity of the different shocks and the impact on growth is treated similar far all shocks. If the current shock is more serious than the previous ones the growth may fall even further.

But some counter-cyclical fiscal measures will surely have to be taken. Perhaps one to be considered seriously is a cut in the central excise duties as this will lower prices and brings forth new demand. This will give greater strength to finance minister's demand for industrialists to reduce prices. Policymakers have to deploy all tools at their command to boost business sentiments and consumer confidence which are both badly shaken. It is an extraordinary situation seeking extraordinary measures.

4

The Global Meltdown and Indian Economic Prospects

THE myth that India had decoupled from the global economy, stated with such bravado by our industrialists and policymakers about a year ago at several international forums including Davos, has been well and truly exploded. The Indian economy is presently faced with a severe downturn that has already seen the year-on-year GDP growth in the third quarter of the fiscal year 2008-09 slumping to 5.3 per cent with the quarter actually recording a zero growth when compared with the previous quarter. The last quarter of this year will do only a shade better because of some improvement in agriculture output. The news on the manufacturing sector looks dismal with commercial vehicles production plummeting by (-)50 per cent in January, exports likely to decline yet again for the fourth month in a row, petroleum imports down by a third and even auto, steel and cement sales in January and February beginning to slacken compared to previous months. The clear writing on the wall is for the GDP growth in 2008-09 being no more than 5 per cent in the second-half of the year. This will imply a GDP growth of between 6-6.5 per cent for 2008-09. Some of our leading policymakers and bankers who still maintain that the economy will achieve a 7 per cent GDP growth in this fiscal year are clearly in a state of denial. Either for electoral or other reasons, they are persisting with the myth of India's invulnerability to its external environment. The assumption seems to be that India continues to be a somewhat insulated economy that can achieve high and

sustained rates of growth on the basis of its domestic demand. This assumption is simply untenable.

It is difficult to fathom the reason for this denial because, to any observer of the Indian economy, the rise in the level of the Indian economy's global integration must be inescapable. As Figure 4.1 shows, the share of the external sector (exports and imports of both merchandise goods and services including software exports and remittances) increased from 19 per cent in 1990-91 to about 52 per cent in 2007-08. This and the nearly threefold increase in the international content of our economic activity gets even more pronounced if we take into consideration capital inflows and outflows which also of course affect the level and direction of economic activity in the country. As some of us who have suffered the meltdown of the Indian equity prices since January 2008 know to our cost, the plunge in stock prices started not because of any negative events in the domestic economy but were a result of the bad news from the US and European economies. The Indian stock markets which have lost more than 70 per cent of its market capitalisation since its peak in January 2008, was brought down principally by the withdrawal of foreign equity

capital by investors pulling out from the Indian market simply to
repatriate capital back home to shore up the sagging balance sheets of their
parent companies.

FIGURE 4.1

**Share of the External Sector (Exports and Imports of
both Merchandise Goods and Services)**

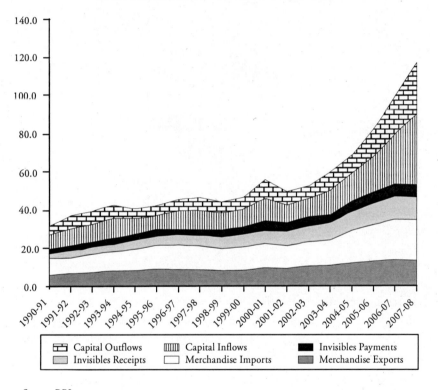

Source: RBI.

The net withdrawal of about $14 billion (nearly Rs. 60,000 crore) of
foreign capital from the Indian stock market in 2008 precipitated the
vapourisation of stock market wealth in the last 13 months, which saw
trillions of rupees of wealth being wiped out from the market. This, in
turn, has severely affected the corporate sector's ability to mobilise
investment, soured investment intentions and significantly slowed down
real estate demand where prices are on a fairly slippery slope. The real

estate downturn is also directly affected by a drop in remittances as oil dependent economies reel from the impact of oil prices gyrating between $146 per barrel at the end of June 2008 to below $40 per barrel now.

FIGURE 4.2

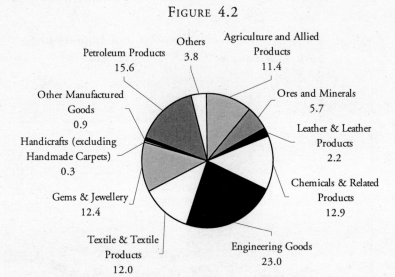

Source: RBI—*Handbook of Indian Statistics.*

Moreover, although the Indian economy's dependence on export demand is much lower than, for example, that of China, our exports have a much higher multiplier effect in the domestic economy. This is because, except for gems and jewellery, ores and minerals and petroleum exports that account for less than 33.7 per cent of the total, the import content of our exports is very small.

Unlike China, which in some sense assembles imports for final exports, the domestic content of India's exports is high. A decline in exports in sectors like textile, garments, engineering goods like auto components or machine tools or software has a significant impact on domestic demand. Thus, a sharp fall in export growth, as has been experienced since October 2008 and is likely to continue in the coming year on account of weak external demand, still has a significant impact on the level of economic activity in the country. Therefore, India, we must all note, is well and truly integrated in the global division of labour and affected by international flows of trade, technology and finance. Unfortunately, this is not sufficiently recognised not only by the majority of our political class, which is expectedly inward looking (only domestic voters matter) but surprisingly also not given sufficient attention by a large segment of our corporate leaders and entrepreneurs. The proof of this lack of appreciation of our external environment is amply evident in the relative lack of attention given to the external environment in the business press. Further evidence is provided by our industry associations in which the role of the international departments, if any at all, is largely restricted to felicitating visiting dignitaries and arranging protocol for visiting business delegations. If Indian industry was oriented towards the external environment, it would ensure that the monitoring and analytical capabilities of their international departments were strengthened so that emerging trends could be tracked and analysed to ensure that Indian corporates could be forewarned and take necessary strategic decisions. This is hardly the case at present and must change if Indian industry is to become globally competitive and achieve its true growth potential.

It is important in this context to understand the nature and full extent of the global crisis that is currently unfolding. Even the head of the US Federal Reserve, Ben Bernanke, has now publicly stated that the current global economic downturn is by far the worst crisis afflicting the centre of global capitalism since the Great Depression of the 1930s. The subprime crisis that started in the latter half of 2007, soon transformed in to a global financial crisis of September 2008 after the US government allowed the collapse of the Lehman Brothers. In future, this one policy mistake, of equal magnitude to the Smoot-Hawley import tariffs in the 1930s because of its effect on business and economic confidence and prospects could be remembered as having precipitated the start of the global downturn. Lehman's collapse froze credit flows, stopped even the commodity markets from operating normally and stopped the equity markets virtually in their tracks. This resulted in the economic environment being characterised by Knightian uncertainty (which does not lend itself to any probabilistic outcomes) and led to the financial crisis morphing itself into an economic downturn in advanced economies. The meltdown in the 'main streets' of the OECD economies has in turn been transmitted through the virtual collapse of global trade to a sharp economic downturn in emerging markets which have seen their manufactured exports collapse and a large scale rise in unemployment. At the same time, commodity prices, including oil prices have plummeted to record lows with more downward movement still expected in coming months.

By allowing the real estate bubble to build up beyond all rational levels and permitting financial agents to grossly under-price risks, the US regulators have unwittingly unleashed the most severe crisis for global capitalism since the 1930s. While the response of developed economies has thankfully been prompt, significant and to some extent coordinated, success in engendering an early global economic recovery is certainly not assured. Already several leading world economists like Paul Krugman and Joseph Stiglitz are critical of the US and European policy response being behind the curve. Given the unprecedented, across-the-board declines in GDP and trade flows in OECD economies in the last quarter of 2008, we may not have yet seen the bottom of this cyclical downturn in the global economy. The nightmare scenario of negative feedback from export-oriented economies like China, East Asia and Central and Southern Europe further aggravating the downturn in the core OECD economies and developing into a vicious downward spiral cannot at this stage be ruled out. This will imply that a full-fledged recovery may not be in our sight until the end of 2010. And this could well be coterminous with an L-shaped economic performance for the US economy which, like Japan in the 90s, could enter into a phase of 'growth recession'. This will have serious implications for India and all other emerging economies. It will be useful for our policymakers to understand the implications of such an eventuality and prepare plans to deal with such outcomes.

The Indian economy has suffered a rather extreme external shock, which may well have some further negative stimuli ahead for us. It was unfortunate that the external shock followed almost immediately on the heels of a sustained bout of monetary policy tightening which saw the RBI raising interest rates and the cash reserve ratio (CRR) as late as August 2008. Thus, the economy already beginning to enter into a policy induced downward phase of the cycle, was faced with a freezing of both national and international credit markets that saw a near complete drying up of liquidity as reflected in the overnight interest rates spiking up to

20 per cent on 26 September. The third quarter of the current fiscal has seen a sharp decline in manufacturing activity with export growth also in negative territory. The GDP growth in the third quarter has come in at 5.3 per cent as compared to 9.4 per cent in the same quarter last year. According to the model of 'LEI', constructed by the team of macroeconomic researchers at ICRIER, the fourth quarter growth in 2008-09 will be below 5 per cent and the overall GDP growth in this fiscal will be no more than 6.4 per cent. As Figure 4.3 shows, the model tracks the Indian GDP growth quite closely. According to this model, which takes into account the external shock by calibrating it on the basis of earlier shocks suffered by the economy, GDP growth in 2009-10 will be about 4 per cent. The first-half (April to September) will achieve only 3.8 per cent growth with a weak recovery starting in the second half and raising the growth to above 4 per cent. Whether we will see the recovery that starts in October 2009 being sustained and gathering strength will depend upon the state of the global economy and the policy measures taken by the new government, which comes in to power at the end of May.

FIGURE 4.3

LEI Model Tracks the Indian GDP Growth

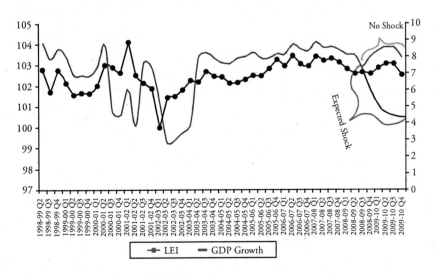

Source: Rajiv Kumar, Mathew Joseph, Dony Alex and Pankaj Vashist.

From all accounts, the OECD economies, including the US, will not see the beginning of a meaningful recovery until well into the second half of 2010. Thus, the external environment for the Indian economy will remain less than benign in the foreseeable future. Growth will, therefore, have to be generated principally either by hugely raising domestic demand or by achieving higher market shares in external markets. Attention would have to be focussed on Asian economies which, though also suffering the impact of the global downturn, are likely to achieve positive growth. In this context, the delay in finalising the Indo-ASEAN free trade agreement could be a major mistake. It is time that Indian industry is driven to become more aggressive rather than try and operate in its relatively protected domestic market.

The scope for stimulating domestic demand through a rise in public expenditures is severely limited in the light of the very high fiscal deficits already. The fiscal deficit in 2008-09 will end up at more than 11 per cent of the GDP, which is the highest since 1992. Even if the next regular budget in July spends an additional 1 per cent of GDP in another stimulus package, the fiscal deficit will rise to 12 per cent. These levels of deficits are clearly unsustainable and will raise the public debt levels to extraordinary levels. This will lead to a deterioration in sovereign ratings and a sharp hike in interest rates at which Indian corporates or for that matter the government will be able to borrow abroad. This will necessitate that the new government seriously pursues disinvestment options, which was completely ignored by the present UPA dispensation. There is simply no other fiscal opening for providing the needed fiscal stimulus to recover the growth momentum. Monetary policy could play a major role in stimulating investment, housing and consumer durables demand. With inflation headed towards the zero level by the beginning of April, the RBI has little reason to keep the interest rate at 5 per cent, especially when global commodity prices are likely to remain soft in the coming months. But the real problem seems to be a lack of demand for credit from the banks, which are now flush with liquidity. Perhaps, a paradigm shift in the operation of commercial banks to enable them to invest directly in productive activities is worth considering at this time. And in any case the reverse repo rate needs to be brought down to zero to take away any incentive for banks to park their monies with the RBI.

The real challenge for Indian policymakers and India Inc. is, however, to try and raise the share of India's exports in major markets and product segments. It is really ironical that India's share in world trade remains at about the same level as in 1950! This is not tenable any longer if we have to achieve rapid growth with equity. Exports have the desirable characteristic of being relatively labour intensive. This is especially true of services exports that include a wide range of exports such as software, tourist earnings and films, accountancy, legal services etc. On the other hand, there is hardly reason for our textile and garment exports to lose ground, as they have been doing, to Bangladesh, Vietnam and other such smaller economies when we still have such a large pool of unemployed human resources. For pushing both services and labour-intensive manufactured exports, policymakers must pay much greater attention to labour market reforms on the one hand and to development of vocational skills on the other. Overall, it is important to emphasise that while fiscal and monetary stimuli may provide the much needed short-term palliatives for shoring up GDP growth, the real push will only come from implementing structural reforms, the agenda for which has really been put on the shelf for a while. We cannot hope to generate the needed economic activity or the employment levels by continuing to tinker around with the economy. Bold and visionary measures, such as those undertaken in the early 1990s, are needed again if the economy is not to slip into a prolonged phase of anaemic growth.

5

The Sky is not Falling yet

THE wolf is at the door. I had written in January that decoupling is a myth. Painfully, we are learning the truth that actions far away, like the El Nino, which happens because the waters of the South Pacific get warmer, affect us here in India. Some urgent actions are, therefore, called for to restore market confidence and prevent investment sentiments from turning sour. The first step economic policy managers must take is to restore their credibility, which, as we know, was the highest any team could ever hope to have. To achieve this, they have to forthrightly reject the dangerous goldilocks Centre for Monitoring Indian Economy (CMIE) story of GDP growth being 9.4 per cent next year. They would do well to say how a short and shallow cyclical downturn is the best we can hope for and that they are focussing now on reforms to raise the potential growth rate to above its current level of 8.5 per cent. Second, they should use the pile of foreign exchange reserves that has been accumulated to intervene in the market and put harder brakes on slowing down the Rupee's slide. I have always favoured a relatively weak currency as it keeps the price of labour relatively cheap and thus helps labour-embodied manufactured or service exports. But the current slide in the Rupee is beginning to seriously affect market sentiment and investor confidence and is nullifying the gains from the softening of oil prices and so action is needed to stop this steep decline. Very often, signals are important and this will be one of them.

Third, while I have not looked at the numbers, clearly a faster unwinding of the market stabilisation scheme (MSS) facility is perhaps called for to introduce greater liquidity in the market. Fourth, a concomitant condition to facilitate liquidity expansion is for the RBI to meet with the financial sector CEOs on a daily basis and identify the causes for the liquidity crunch and ensure, with their help, that overnight rates are prevented from shooting up unexpectedly. This step will minimise surprises, improve anticipation and show to the markets that RBI has its hand firmly on the rudder. Fifth, following the Chinese and South African Central Banks lead, the authorities can signal that circumstances require a higher threshold for inflation and, in any case, with global commodity prices and oil prices on a southward trend, the pressures are gone and we can expect a more benign inflationary situation in the months to come. This will prevent outcries from misguided 'inflation targeters' against expanding liquidity. Sixth, the government should direct the Department of Industrial Policy and Promotion (DIPP) to come out with inflation numbers once a month henceforth.

I am hoping this will not violate any constitutional or statutory provisions. Seventh, and last, the government must announce, as it did in the case of scotching negative market rumours against ICICI, that all bank deposits or other financial savings in the provident fund, insurance policies etc., are safe and guaranteed. I know these are protected but the last thing we need at this stage is for depositors to get cold feet and start a run even on a small private bank somewhere. Make this announcement and let those who talk of costs of moral hazard etc., discuss this with the US Treasury Secretary who has shown us the way!

Some structural factors make us less vulnerable to the turmoil in global financial markets. First, our banking sector is only marginally integrated with global flows and financial exclusion is so widespread that the real economy will not be disastrously affected. It will be affected by weakening external demand but that will happen with a lag. Second, in sharp contrast to China, net exports contribute a negative 10.5 per cent to our current GDP growth, domestic investment (57 per cent) and consumption (53 per cent). This makes us less vulnerable. Finally, the private economy in India, including the infamous parallel economy, remains hugely surplus. Starting from unaccounted payments for real estate to gold purchases and consumption of services, this will buoy up domestic demand. So the sky is not falling down yet! Policymakers need to highlight these and take cognisance of these and other India-specific factors. An 'Indian strategy' for achieving growth with macro stability has to be crafted by putting together heads from the government, industry and the academia.

6

Time to Play it Cool

THE Indian stock markets have crashed and went in to free fall on Friday, 24th October 2008. Surely not the sort of year ending that Hindu businessmen were looking for as they close their books and welcome Lakshmi, in the new year. Most observers were quick to lay the blame at RBI's door because its credit policy announcement left all major rates unchanged and made it look disconnected to the ongoing equity meltdown. By late night as the Governor's explanations came in and surely by Saturday morning the tone had changed. People could see that the Friday massacre on Dalal street had more to do with the negative sentiment globally rather than only reflecting RBI having ignored market expectations.

Before approaching important policy issues, let me address the issue of the equity meltdown. I have written in the past, and still maintain, that policymakers should not react to equity market changes as these do not reflect real policy concerns. If foreign institutional investors (FIIs) are selling at any price and are willing to suffer the combined loss of price discounts and exchange rate depreciation, then so be it. In fact, this provides opportunities for bargain hunting by domestic investors. However, beyond some levels, the continued fall in stock prices can negatively affect both investor and consumer sentiment and seriously erode people's confidence in the market itself. This must be avoided by any means as entrepreneurs' 'animal spirits' take very long to emerge from such a crisis. Therefore, the government and RBI have to prevent markets from

falling below a particular level even if this is achieved by direct intervention as was done by the Hong Kong Monetary Authority, HKMA (with the intrepid Andrew Sheng in command) in 1998 in the midst of the Asian financial crisis. HKMA directly bought up large volumes of plummeting stocks, shored up the market and then made a killing when markets perked up later. It is perhaps time to prepare such a plan here at this time and announce its preparation in advance. This in itself will calm the heavily stressed markets.

Policymakers are currently faced simultaneously with all three concerns of a higher than acceptable inflation level, a slowdown in economic growth and financial sector instability. This calls for a very fine balancing act that is not easy to achieve. In addition, there are still nagging concerns that liquidity remains tight although overnight interest rates have now declined below the repo rate at which banks can borrow from the RBI. Some banks are even depositing cash with the RBI reflecting easier liquidity conditions. But that liquidity is still tight is perhaps reflected more in the weekly and monthly interest rates, which remain in double digits and reflect more the liquidity conditions rather than credit risk.

Liquidity is tight not as much due to withdrawal by FIIs, which is a contributing factor, but due to Indian banks now being asked to provide foreign currency cover for their domestic clients to meet their overseas obligations arising from acquisitions abroad by Indian corporates or commodity purchases for which necessary funds are not being advanced by their foreign banks. Secondly, banks overseas are also refusing to provide the usual trade financing, which again has to be provided by domestic banks. Both actions not only suck out rupee liquidity but have directly contributed to the rapid depreciation of the rupee which has sunk about 25 per cent in less than two months, an unacceptably sharp decline that affects investors' confidence. Moreover, liquidity remains tight also because of financing requirements of oil importing companies who continue to rely on bank borrowings until they actually get hold of the funds sanctioned recently by the Parliament. Therefore, it would have been useful for the RBI to have announced another 1 per cent cut in the CRR which would have still remained at 5.5 per cent, leaving sufficient room for further action if so warranted.

There is a case also for further reduction in the repo rate to signal RBI's intent that, in the given circumstances of extraordinary financing burdens on domestic banks, it is not averse to a credit growth higher than its target of 20 per cent. It is important for the RBI to carefully examine the sectoral distribution of non-food credit so that it can figure out if credit growth is adequately financing real economy investment needs. I cannot see how these two steps of lowering the CRR by 1 per cent and the repo rate by 50 basis points, could have harmed the objectives of keeping inflation reined in and improving financial stability. They would have surely had a growth impetus and kept policy ahead of the curve. At the same time, the markets would not have felt so let down. But it would be churlish to fault the newly appointed Governor, already going through an initiation by fire, for having missed an opportunity this time.

7

Headed for a Soft Landing?

THE latest numbers show that the GDP growth rate in the first quarter of 2008-09 has declined to 7.9 per cent from 9.6 per cent in the first quarter last year. While this is the slowest in the past three years, it is pretty good news, coming in the face of all the monetary tightening that the Reserve Bank of India (RBI) has been attempting in the past 18 months. It is also in line with ICRIER's forecast of 7.8 per cent for the full year, based on our model of leading indicators.

A growth rate that is close to the potential growth rate of 8-8.5 per cent, as estimated by more than one agency, shows successful policy intervention in cooling the economy and hopefully avoiding a further exacerbation of inflationary expectations. With the economic slowdown and a marked softening of global oil prices, the worst of the inflationary pressures may well be behind us.

The two important questions are, whether the GDP growth will continue at this lower, but eminently acceptable rate of around 7-7.5 per cent in the coming two years (2009-10 and 2010-11). This will indicate a very shallow downturn and should be a cause of all round cheer. At the same time, the slowdown in the current year could well be the beginning of a downward cycle, which may take the economy to much lower growth rates of 4-5 per cent, as in all previous downturns. That will, of course, be disastrous.

The second question is whether it is possible, like in China, for India to raise its potential growth rate to higher levels of 10-12 per cent. This

will enable the Indian economy to sustain double digit growth without causing inflationary episodes. A closer look at major sector performances can give us some idea of the likely depth and duration of the downward phase of the cycle. Central Statistical Organisation (CSO) numbers show that growth in all the major sectors—agriculture, industry, manufacturing, and services—is lower in the first quarter of this year compared with the first quarter of 2007-08. The most marked decline is in manufacturing, where the growth has come down to 5.6 per cent from 10.9 per cent. More worryingly, this is the second quarter in succession when manufacturing growth has come in below 6 per cent. This across-the-board slowdown can lead us to a deeper trough at the slightest push from a poor agriculture performance or a slowdown in the global economy. At this stage, therefore, the economy can be seen to be on a rather thin ice. Construction is the only sector where growth in the first quarter this year, at 11.4 per cent, has been higher than in the first quarter last year, when it grew at 7.7 per cent. This is particularly surprising as real estate is an interest-sensitive sector. May be the finance ministry's strategy of shielding smaller housing loans from interest rate hikes is working. Also, public sector outlays, which are not interest-rate sensitive, are helping to sustain growth in physical infrastructure sectors.

Construction has significant backward linkages and also has a weight of about 9 per cent in GDP. Sustaining higher growth rates in this sector could be the main plank of a countercyclical government fiscal policy. However, with the fiscal deficit numbers going through the roof on account of farm loan waivers, oil, fertiliser and food subsidy and the coming impact of the Sixth Pay Commission, there is simply no scope for any such countercyclical fiscal policy stance. Despite the finance ministry's advice, commercial banks cannot be expected to keep interest rates on hold for long, even for small housing loans. Therefore, construction sector growth will also likely head downwards in the coming quarters.

Past experience in India and other countries shows that the housing and real estate sectors are typically characterised by a wider swing in growth cycles. So, a decline in demand and growth rates in this sector can be expected to persist for some quarters and also go down more sharply. The performance of this sector in the next couple of quarters will be a strong indicator of the nature of the downward cycle. The industrial slowdown is quite marked and looks to be getting entrenched. The decline has now continued over the past five quarters. With a 26 per cent weight in GDP, this has strong potential to pull down the overall growth rate to unacceptably low levels. A pick-up in export growth could offset this declining trend and raise manufacturing sector growth on the basis of external demand. However, export growth in India has been driven largely by growth in petroleum product exports, which really are quite unconnected with the rest of the economy. The recent depreciation of the rupee is, however, a good sign. This is one area in which public policy can make a real difference by taking the required steps to simplify export procedures and take up trade facilitation measures. These will not only reduce transaction costs, but also give a real push to our small and medium exporters, for whom these procedures represent a real barrier in entering export markets. Without a substantial pick-up in the manufacturing sector, based as it will have to be on external demand, we cannot hope that the downturn will be shallow or short. The government should, therefore, focus its efforts on raising growth rates in the construction sector and in manufactured exports if a soft landing is to be achieved.

8

A Counter-Inflation Subsidy

IT will be very surprising if the Reserve Bank of India (RBI) does not signal a tightening of its policy stance on 29 January. I expect that given the huge liquidity overhang, the cash reserve ratio (CRR) will be raised by between 25 and 50 basis points. I doubt if the repo or the reverse repo will be raised, but will not be completely surprised if that happened because RBI has more updated data on a worsening consumer inflation situation.

With the wholesale price index (WPI) threatening to get into double digits, RBI will be justified in acting decisively to prevent inflationary expectations from becoming entrenched. A tightening of monetary policy when the economy is beginning to get out of its downturn and credit growth and investment demand are anaemic will surely have an adverse effect on investment demand even if banks maintain lending rates. A hardening of interest rates will not only dampen investment intentions but also attract more capital inflows. This will exert upward pressure on the rupee's exchange rate, adversely affecting exports, which are just recovering from a 12-month-long decline. Could all this have been avoided?

The answer is yes. We could have avoided putting the entire onus of countering inflation on monetary policy by taking measures to tackle food inflation that has been raging in the double digits for several months. We have instead the unseemly spectacle of blame and counter-blame between the Union and state governments and within the Union government itself.

The agriculture ministry is blamed for mishandling the situation and the latter passes the buck back by stating that the entire cabinet is responsible for tackling price rise. This is rather disingenuous because it is the responsibility of the agriculture minister to take the necessary initiatives and exert pressure on his cabinet colleagues to move in the desired direction. Everyone seems to have simply resigned to an improvement in the *rabi* harvest to bring down food prices. Such policy paralysis does not inspire confidence.

The durable and effective solution to the phenomenon of rising food prices will come from raising agriculture yields, which have been stagnating for decades, and improving productivity levels by pumping more investment into rural infrastructure and introducing new technology. There is a growing gap between rising per capita income and declining per capita availability of food products. This gap can be filled by raising domestic output, facilitating movement of agricultural produce across state borders and liberalising agricultural imports and exports. These will allow private traders to respond in a timely and effective manner to tackle emerging shortages and prevent price increases. But these are medium- to long-term measures.

More immediately, we must start by taking a clear view on factors that are responsible for rising food prices. Demand has picked up with higher purchasing power in the hands of the poor through the National Rural Employment Guarantee Act (NREGA) and other social security expenditures and the expanding middle classes. Supply shortages have emerged due to the drought and stagnating yields, and these are exacerbated by speculative activity fuelled by excessive liquidity, which also feeds on itself. The only possible remedy appears to be the import of relatively large quantities of lentils, cereals, sugar and edible oils that are usually the main culprits. These imports can be supplied to the open market at lower than currently prevailing prices. The government has to announce its firm intention to persist with such imports even if that involves a measure of subsidy, as the landed prices of imports could well be higher than prices at which these additional supplies can be introduced in the domestic market. It should also announce that it will continue with these subsidised, open market operations until food prices come down and inflationary expectations have been reversed.

Such an 'inflation-countering subsidy' is justified as a vital input for maintaining growth with macroeconomic stability. At the same time, a roadmap for restoring fiscal balances over the next 3 to 5 years will signal that both fiscal and monetary policies are being directed to suck out excess liquidity from the system. That will help dampen speculative activity.

What could possibly be the problem with such a move? The most pernicious argument I have heard is that the government should allow traders to make extra profits in times of relative scarcity when in times of relative abundance they are forced to incur losses because the government does not lift export bans in time and stops procurement activities. It is time we took an urgent and serious look at liberating Indian agriculture from the extensive government controls that are in place, ostensibly to protect our small and marginal farmers. I am convinced that with limited, well-targeted and market-based government interventions, both small farmers and consumers will benefit from a greater integration of Indian agriculture with global markets and greater access to foreign technology and capital flows.

9

Three Critical Reform Priorities

WITH the new government due to take office hopefully soon, it is now open season for offering ideas, advice and suggestions for policy reforms. We are all very good at giving advice and don't really bother if most of it goes unheeded. It is crucial in my view to retain the policy focus on the most critical issues to give them some sense of urgency and priority. Drawing up a long list of desirable actions can often end up in virtual policy paralysis due to the inevitable trade-offs among the objectives and not enough implementation capacity. Therefore, I want to focus only on three critical measures and let others reiterate the necessity of more fiscal stimulus despite the limited headroom—improving infrastructure; restarting the disinvestment programme; introducing GSP (generalised system of preferences); expanding electricity generation and so on.

I want to focus on three elements that in my view deserve the most urgent attention if we are not to lose the plot and see the much-hyped demographic dividend get morphed into a demographic nightmare, as the numbers of rising unemployed youth swell the ranks of militant organisations that peddle either bogus religious fundamentalism or defunct Left-wing extremist ideology. The rise of extremist ideologies and movements in India is a real danger that any incoming government will be well advised to take seriously.

First, it must be recognised that the central and, I daresay, the exclusive focus of government policy should be to sustain high economic

growth of not less than 8 per cent for the next two decades. All political parties and economic pundits can hopefully converge on this one central policy objective. Let us also agree that achieving rapid and sustained growth, while being necessary, is not a sufficient condition for reducing poverty and certainly not for addressing rising inequities in the country. To achieve these necessary objectives of inclusive growth, relevant policy measures will have to be taken. But it is important for us to build a nation-wide consensus on achieving high rates of economic growth, as that alone can ensure that we achieve any of our desired and stated objectives.

The second element that needs utmost attention is to qualitatively improve the delivery of public goods and services, starting with law and order. It is time we firmly rejected forever the nonsensical notion that the 'Indian economy can grow despite the government.' This is sillier than believing that our economy is decoupled from the global economy.

I am told that one of the fastest growing industries in the country today is 'provision of private security'. If this is a fact, it should shock all of us and any self-respecting government should be embarrassed to recognise that we have privatised the maintenance of law and order except for the VVIPs. This must change if we are to have any claims of being a modern civil society. *Slumdog Millionaire* may have won the Oscars, but its depiction of the treatment that the hero receives at the police station must make all of us hang our heads in shame.

The other crucial aspect is the delivery of public education. It is in shambles. There is as yet no consensus on how to improve this. Installing video cameras to record teachers' attendance and performance may produce good results in laboratory-like situations, but can this possibly be implemented on the scale required? And are we sure that a way around it will not be found by those who have no incentive in the success of the system. What is wrong with experimenting with education vouchers on a large scale? They will empower the beneficiaries, provide the needed competition to government schools, which, at present, have a local monopoly, and cut at the very root of the 'private tuition industry' that is full of unwanted practices. Education vouchers should be launched as soon as possible.

The third priority must be to rejuvenate Indian agriculture and ensure that 4 per cent growth is sustained over the next decade with further diversification and productivity improvement. For this, we need to tackle the binding constraints that agriculture is faced with today. These, in my view, are the small size of land holdings; absence of any real extension services to bring in new technologies and provide market information; exclusion of rural households from commercial bank credit; complete misuse of chemical fertilisers and pesticides; lack of any accountability of government and public sector petty officials who operate in the countryside and inadequate supply of electricity. All these have to be tackled on a war footing. Raising yields and productivity in agriculture is essential for achieving inclusive growth. The incoming government should come out with a white paper that evaluates the success of the measures taken in the past five years and spells out others required to address binding constraints. This should be done within the first 100 days. After country-wide consultations, it should be converted into an action plan and implemented in a mission mode. It is time to recognise that the woes of our small and marginal farmers have very little to do with the WTO negotiations on agriculture and a lot to do with outdated and dysfunctional policies that are still prevalent in this sector.

10

Time to Consolidate Reforms

THE latest *World Economic Outlook* (WEO), IMF's flagship publication, focusses on the global financial crisis and its impact on the real economy. It has revised downwards its forecasts made in July 2008 with the global economy now expected to grow only by 3.9 per cent in 2008 and 3.0 per cent in 2009, which officially makes for a global recession next year. GDP in advanced economies is expected to rise by an anaemic 1.5 per cent in 2008 and 0.5 per cent in 2009. Emerging economies are expected to maintain a growth of 6.9 per cent in 2008 and a lower 6.1 per cent in 2009. This is nearly 2 percentage points down from the previous two years when emerging economies had registered an 8 per cent economic growth with the world output rising by 5 per cent in both 2006 and 2007. Chinese growth rate is expected to come down to 9.7 and 9.3 per cent in 2008 and 2009, while India's GDP is estimated to increase by nearly 8 per cent and 7 per cent in these two years. World trade, according to WEO, is still expected to achieve a positive growth of 5 and 4 per cent in these two years.

These numbers reveal a sharp and across-the-board slowing down of the global economy, largely as a result of the financial sector meltdown that we have witnessed since September 2008 when Lehman Brothers was allowed to collapse. The more worrying aspect of these forecasts is that they are probably already out of date and need to be revised downwards again. For starters, the World Bank has already forecast that world trade growth will be negative this year. From all the news coming out of the

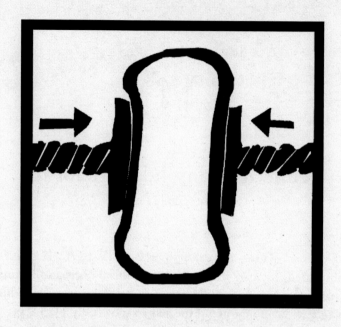

US, it is clear that it has been in recession since December 2007, which implies that WEO's estimate of US growth of 1.6 per cent in 2008 is overly optimistic. With house prices still declining, construction at a near stand still and unemployment numbers worsening with each successive week, it now seems that US economy could contract by as much as 5 per cent in the fourth quarter of 2008. This will, in all likelihood, imply that the US economy will perhaps remain recession bound even in 2009 despite the trillion dollar stimulus package, reportedly under consideration of the new administration. The UK and Germany, the two largest economies in the Euro zone, are also likely to see negative growth in 2009. And Japan, with its exports in November 2008 plunging 26 per cent over the same month in 2007, is likely to be recession bound in 2009. The news coming out of China also points to a sharper decline in their exports and GDP growth than is forecast in the latest WEO. I will, therefore, not be surprised to see the advanced economies actually experience a real contraction and see their GDP decline in 2009. With large emerging economies also now expected to grow much slower, we will be fortunate if the global economy registers a positive rate of growth in 2009. Indeed, tough years ahead.

This implies a very weak external demand for India and other emerging economies. India is not as dependent on external demand for its growth impetus as, for example, is China where exports account for 40 per cent of the GDP as compared to India's 23 per cent (including both goods and services). But with a very low consumption ratio and high import ratio, China's income multiplier is lower than India's. Therefore, the contribution of exports to GDP may not be much lower in India in comparison with China. Merchandise exports have been growing at 31 per cent till September 2008. Software exports grew by 21 per cent till Q1: 2008-09 and remittances by over 50 per cent. However, export growth slowed down sharply in September 2008 and turned negative by a large 12 per cent in October. Export growth could fall to 10 per cent or below in 2008 and next year due to the weak global economy. This could by itself seriously bring down the GDP growth in 2009.

Therefore, any forecast for the Indian economy, that puts 2009-10 growth rate for the Indian economy at higher than in 2008-09 sounds rather incredible. And to forecast near 8 per cent growth in 2009-10, as some senior official economists have apparently done, is perhaps irresponsible. Indian investors would be better advised to completely discount such wild optimism. They should instead consolidate their capacities and try to become more competitive in preparation for the next upturn that could hopefully start in 2010. It is never inevitable that high savings rate like 33 per cent in India and 53 per cent in China will produce high growth rates. High savings rates can simply result in growing bank deposits and worsening deposit to credit ratios as Japan has seen over a decade. Economies suffer from excess capacity expansion that does not generate output. Economies also export away their savings as reflected in current account surpluses, which, for China, is estimated by the IMF to be at about 9 per cent of GDP in 2009!

I think Indian policymakers are less sanguine about 2009 growth prospects as is reflected in the official encouragement to recalcitrant commercial banks to reduce lending rates and in offering incentives to exporters and small house owners. We need to continue with these growth stimulating policies and focus also on structural reforms to ensure that economic growth recovers in the second-half of 2009. The first half of next year will perhaps see a less than 5 per cent growth and so a recovery in the second-half of next year is the best we can hope for.

11

Focus on Follow-up

TWO news items on Monday caught my attention. The first reported Ratan Tata's views that the Investment Commission (IC), which he headed, should be wound up principally because of lack of follow-up on its recommendations. The second item quoted the commerce and industry minister as saying that the government is likely to announce a new manufacturing policy by the end of March, and that in his view the share of the manufacturing sector in India's gross domestic product should increase from the present 16 per cent to 25 per cent. Bravo!

But do we really need another brand new policy for the manufacturing sector to push up its growth rate? We already have the recommendations of the IC, most of which, according to Tata himself, have not been implemented. Not only that, we also have several reports, including the 'National Strategy for Manufacturing' from the National Manufacturing Competitiveness Council (NMCC) and a comprehensive set of recommendations in the industry chapter of the Eleventh Plan. Plus we have an assortment of recommendations in reports from think tanks and industry associations. Clearly, we can hardly complain about a dearth of ideas and recommendations to promote manufacturing growth. In fact, the attempt should be to drastically reduce the number of procedures and requirements and to focus attention on implementing the recommendations that address the most binding constraints. At the least, any new policy document would do well to include a list of recommendations received over the last five years and give us an action-

taken report, including the recommendations that have been consciously rejected.

For example, it can be shown that with cumulative foreign direct investment (FDI) inflows in the last four years crossing $85 billion, we have already achieved IC's recommendation of attracting $72 billion as FDI in the five years starting 2006-07 and also exceeded the annual target of $15 billion with FDI inflows crossing $27 billion in 2008-09. Yet, it seems only less than 40 per cent of these inflows are destined for the manufacturing sector in India, compared with more than two-thirds in China. While not detracting from this amazing turnaround (FDI inflows in 2005-06 were hardly $5 billion and the total FDI in the previous decade was a mere $16.7 billion), we must ask ourselves how much of this was because of global factors such as investors trying to diversify country risk away from China, and the 'good India story' made to look even better in the context of the global recession, and what could honestly be attributed to measures taken to improve the domestic environment for FDI and investment, in general. Would it not be a fair assessment to say that the spurt in FDI flows during the last four years has happened despite the lack of any real reform and not because of them? One of the first steps, already in the pipeline it appears, would be to rationalise the number of press notes while putting them together and reduce them to a handful that can still address all major concerns.

At present, these press notes and other notifications, with their inevitably varying interpretations and the plethora of procedures and licences, create a virtual maze which can be tackled only by those who have 'heels of iron' to run around the corridors and 'pockets of gold' to pay the 'consultants' and lawyers. This restricts the pool to the large multinationals and excludes the small and medium foreign investors from the mid-west in the US or the Kansai region in Japan or the Ruhr in Germany, who are constantly on the lookout for cheaper locations and lower wages, pressed as they are in an increasingly competitive global market. We could miss the opportunity of foreign investment moving out of China for a number of reasons, if we do not implement the necessary measures now. Already, Vietnam and Cambodia are attracting increasing volumes, while India's actual and untapped potential for attracting FDI remains under-exploited. Is it an exaggeration to argue that proper follow-up and implementation of existing recommendations would help India surpass China as an investment destination, especially when Japanese firms are beginning to prefer India as an investment destination over China?

So it may be useful to focus attention on implementing some of the more critical reforms that have already been recommended rather than announce a new set of policy objectives. A focus on implementation will bring greater credibility for the government and immense relief to the investors. It will reduce the uncertainty facing the entrepreneurs and strengthen 'animal spirits'. By contrast, announcing 'dedicated investment and manufacturing zones' as part of a new policy, for example, will only create one more scheme which will, most likely, be indistinguishable from several that already exist. It will create another set of enclaves, divert policy attention, fragment governance capacity and confuse potential investors. Will it not be far more fruitful to focus on follow-up, implementation and rationalisation than announce a new policy?

Section II

Reforms are still needed

12

Reviving Manufacturing

CHINA'S manufacturing boom and export surge was in large part a result of the subsidisation of producers through cheap capital, low wages and disciplined labour, combined with the latest technology brought in by foreign direct investment. The People's Liberation Army (PLA) regularly places orders on emerging domestic enterprises to generate economies of scale and be globally competitive. They also transfer technology to these firms. Local governments acquire land for both domestic and foreign enterprises and often contribute the proceeds as equity capital, thereby becoming partners and assuring the investors against any future political risk.

Can India follow the same model? Clearly not in its entirety. However, the land acquisition law, inherited from colonial days, can be immediately junked and replaced with one that enables our farmers to have a direct stake in the venture for which the land was purchased directly by the entrepreneur. But the Chinese model for pushing manufacturing sector growth may not have been sustainable had the US not obliged with an extraordinary increase in its current account deficit. And the model does look susceptible. So which is the way ahead for India? Before I answer that question, I want to give a real-life story.

Metro Playing Card Co. was established in Mumbai in 1948 by a young man, who like a million others had landed a few years earlier in Bombay, penniless and without any connections. His diligence led the firm to prosper and it became one of the leading playing card

manufacturers in the country. During the 1980s, it established a plant
in Nepal as well. Then in January 2005, the family's second generation
shifted the entire production to Yuwe in Hangzhou province in China!
They had stoically borne the difficulties of an erratic power supply, calls
by the inspectors, logistics problems and inadequate credit for five
decades. The trigger to shift was the refusal by its workers—who had been
recently unionised by a rising regional party—to learn new skills and
adopt modern technology, without which Metro could not hope to remain
competitive against cheap imports from China. So Metro decided to
become an importer and rentier instead. It now procures all its supplies
from Yuwe, at a comfortable and clear 14 per cent return per container
of imports (no questions asked!). At the same time, it earns Rs. 8 lakh
a month as rental income. This example, which captures the story of the
ongoing hollowing out of India's manufacturing sector, is unfortunately
not an isolated one. Manufacturing capacities are being routinely shifted
out of India. This trend will surely accelerate as we sign more free trade
agreements (FTAs) allowing zero-duty imports. Many potential domestic
investors are simply not even bothering to start ventures in India, and

like the Mittals, they are looking to other countries as possible locations. The worrying part is that no one seems to care whether it is the small guys such as Metro or the conglomerates such as Mittal, Sony, Infosys and Wipro which prefer to establish capacities abroad rather than in India. Instead, we tend to bask in the glory of our non-resident successful talents. I know that even those who had so far strongly resisted the idea of Indian capital and talent being used to generate employment abroad when our own poverty and unemployment levels are so high are now finally succumbing to 'phoren' attractions. They are being driven out by the difficult investment climate at home. If this trend of conversion of entrepreneurs to rentiers and importers continues, India will certainly be unable to absorb the rising tide of educated but unemployed youth in value-adding jobs. The fabled demographic dividend could be converted into a nightmare in a short time.

But this can be prevented. We need to pay urgent and focussed attention to improving the investment climate in the country. The issues to be tackled are too well-known to merit repetition here. But one which is often not discussed is the manner in which we effectively tax our corporate and producer sectors to subsidise consumers. Industrial electricity tariffs are higher because they are used to cross-subsidise domestic consumers. Railway freight charges are used to subsidise passenger travel. Petrol and diesel prices are higher so that cooking gas and kerosene can be subsidised. Interest rates cannot be brought down because the government must run a huge fiscal deficit to fund subsidies directed at raising consumption. The deficit pre-empts national savings and keeps market interest rates high. All this is done in the name of the poor when the beneficiaries are clearly only the middle class. To this, we should add the transaction costs that result from the plethora of dysfunctional procedures and governance. Do we seriously believe that manufacturing can achieve global competitiveness under these conditions? I have heard senior policymakers argue that it does not matter if growth comes from manufacturing or service industries such as software, Bollywood or tourism. I hope readers will see the dangerous fallacy in this line of thinking.

13

Minimising Uncertainty

THE rapid and sustained growth of manufacturing is a necessary condition for not only generating the required employment for our young workforce, but also for modernising our society and eliminating the dualism—stark differences between the organised and unorganised sector—that currently characterises our economy. Too much reliance on financial and information technology-enabled services could actually produce the opposite results by creating enclaves and exacerbating the dualism.

So this objective of accelerating the growth of manufacturing, increasing its share in India's gross domestic product (GDP) and eliminating the dualism must form one of the cornerstones of our economic policy. Let me note right away that it is very difficult to achieve a consensus on any policy objective in our country, given our diverse vested interests and perspectives. This inhibits policy formulation and implementation and often engenders policy paralysis with deleterious consequences. Hopefully, there will be universal agreement across ideological and political lines on the promotion of manufacturing as a central policy objective both at the Centre and in the states. Given the critical nature of this issue for economic prosperity and social stability, the Inter-State Council could consider convening a special session to forge a formal consensus on this across states.

The issue is how to achieve the required 13-14 per cent annual rate of manufacturing growth in order to raise its share in GDP, and at least

prevent it from declining below the unacceptable 16-17 per cent of our output that it is now. That this rather ambitious growth rate target is eminently achievable can be seen by noting that in some growth nodes—such as the National Capital Region (NCR), the Vadodara-Surat-Ahmedabad belt, the Mumbai-Pune-Nashik and Hosur-Chennai-Coimbatore regions—such manufacturing growth rates are already being achieved and even exceeded. The National Manufacturing Competitiveness Council (NMCC) would do well to study the developments of these rapidly growing manufacturing hubs with the objective of identifying the principal drivers and conditions which have enabled such growth dynamism. These drivers and conditions can be replicated, with necessary adaptations to suit the local environment, elsewhere in the country. This will perhaps be more effective than to continue trying to identify labour-intensive sectors and design packages for their growth and expansion.

The crucial difference in the two approaches is that the first attempts to identify the underlying structural and thematic 'drivers' that promote rapid growth, while the latter approach tries to identify specific sectors or, in a sense, pick winners on the wrong assumption that these can be promoted across the country—irrespective of marked differences in the underlying structural conditions and endowments. It is clear to me that industrial policy in any form is unworkable in a country as diverse as ours and, in any case, the objective of policy should be to create overall growth-promoting conditions rather than to identify sectors.

Another overriding aim should be to reduce uncertainty for potential investors. Uncertainty is different from risk, which the entrepreneur is trained to deal with. Uncertainty arises when we cannot assign any probability to expected outcomes. An example would be the 'change of land use' (CLU) that nearly all prospective manufacturing units have to obtain. This should be a routine matter but is clearly not, as is reflected in major celebrations by the beneficiary on receiving CLU. The reason is that the outcome—despite connections, bribes and knowledge of the inside track—is completely unpredictable. The worst cut is that it can be reversed in the future as well. Such uncertainty is a sure killer of any animal spirits. It is really remarkable that private investment continues under these conditions. For this, we must salute our entrepreneurs who simply do not take no for an answer.

Uncertainty can only be reduced if we minimise the number of conditions manufacturing units have to comply with. At present, the attempt is to have norms on paper that cover the entire panoply of international best practices, simply unachievable in a poor economy such as ours. The only purpose these norms serve is to generate bribes and corruption and 'keep them in line'.

The only four requirements that I think have to be strictly enforced are: not employing child labour; not using female workforce in conditions that compromise their dignity; working conditions that do not damage health; and operating only after having obtained sales and excise tax registrations. This ensures that units do not remain part of the shadow economy, which can be a security risk. Beyond these four conditions, which I guess are not obtained by more than two-thirds of our production units, the government should review the existing laws for jettisoning them forthwith.

Finally, the rationale for manufacturing units having to take advance clearances is not clear. The benchmarks can be listed on the Internet and otherwise for compliance under the threat of exemplary punishments. This works in enforcing other laws and should work in achieving compliance of minimally essential industrial norms.

14

Lessons from Korea

LAST week I went back to Seoul after 26 years. The city is transformed and so is the economy. In 1984, when I visited the export processing zones, Masan and Iri contributed at least 60 per cent of total exports from South Korea. Posco had been established as a public sector company to take on established global giants and outcompeted all of them despite having to import 100 per cent of its raw materials by relying on latest technology, economies of scale and above all, sheer hard work and dedication. And at the same time, Korea was reaching full employment levels by furiously expanding labour-intensive exports. The question arose in my mind that if Korea could successfully combine latest technology with large-scale employment generation, could we do it as well?

The most striking memory from 26 years ago is of having lunch with the president of the Federation of Korean Industries (FKI), the organisation of the Korean *chaebols*, who like the Japanese *zaibatsus*, worked closely with their respective governments to create the two industrial juggernauts. I had asked the president, a wise old man, most gracious in his hospitality to a young researcher, what the main lessons were for India from the Korean experience in industrialisation. He gave me three nuggets that have since remained with me.

First, he said, countries and/or their firms cannot succeed in a fiercely competitive global economy (this was in 1984) unless industry and government worked closely together to achieve national goals.

Second, developing countries should not be unduly concerned about national pride and national brands as long as they can generate the necessary employment for a young workforce by successfully attracting the necessary technology and foreign direct investment (FDI). But they should not forget that both regaining national pride and building national brands are worthy goals to be achieved over time. The Koreans, in their pragmatism had handed over Masan largely to firms from Japan, a country which had colonised Korea not so long ago and had broken down the gate of their emperor's palace so that it did not face in an auspicious direction. Quite rightly, the Koreans are restoring it to its original location ahead of the Group of Twenty summit in November.

Third, that any country is as good as its human capital. He cited with approval the efforts of his friend Prof. Choi, founder of the Korea Advanced Institute of Science and Technology (now KAIST) to bring Korean researchers back from the US by paying them higher salaries than was being paid at that time either to senior bureaucrats or corporate managers. And as we know, Prof. Choi succeeded brilliantly. Korea has emerged as a leader in several frontline technologies and now competes through product innovation and not as a low-cost producer.

Have we learnt these simple lessons in India? I am afraid not. The government and the industry, though not mutually suspicious any more, still do not seem to work together with a common national purpose. For example, maximising employment generation can be a common goal for the government and industry. In this case, special economic zones (SEZs), which have already generated large-scale employment, will hopefully not remain controversial. The criterion for making land available on a priority basis would then become a minimum number of jobs generated per unit of land. All restrictions, except on strategic grounds, would be removed from FDI when it is seen to generate employment.

There is, of course, give and take between the government and industry. But it is often non-transparent and perceived to be largely for private, not national, purpose. This can change if industry decides to make the government accountable and not continue to act as a supplicant seeking favours. But for that, industry has to achieve even greater social legitimacy by paying its taxes honestly, not cutting regulatory corners, and generating employment and lowering prices when it can. It has to be seen by the people as working for national goals and not only in maximising personal consumption and ostentation.

Unlike Korea, we have still not recognised the importance of attracting back our human capital. Instead, we celebrate whenever a person of Indian origin earns global recognition. This is a loser's pride! Given that the Indian higher education system is hardly producing any globally comparable researchers, the only way forward is to attract talent back from abroad as seed capital. Indian industry can play a major role by letting charity begin at home rather than donating millions of dollars to foreign universities.

Moreover, it should be recognised by all those concerned that talent will not be attracted only because of its love for the motherland or for a possible entry into policymaking, increasingly difficult as it is. Researchers need living and working conditions comparable with ones they are giving up. It is time we paid attention to these issues. For once, we can learn from Pakistan, where in 2006, the government announced education pay scales that, in purchasing power parity (PPP) terms, are better than those obtained in most advanced economies!

15

Farm Fresh from Argentina

I write this from Cataratas, the Argentine province bordering Brazil and Paraguay, home to the world-famous Iguazu waterfalls. These are far more spectacular than North America's Niagara Falls. Argentina, with its Evita Peron and Madres de Mayo, has fascinated me for long for several reasons. But during this first visit, two aspects strike me as being particularly relevant for us in India.

First, this nation clearly demonstrates how a domestic elite and its political class, when motivated exclusively by narrow and selfish interests, can drag down even as naturally rich a country as Argentina. Ranked among the 10 richest countries in the world until the 1930s, it is now a struggling middle-income laggard, compared with the European and North American economies that were once its peers. We face this risk in India today and must act to avoid it.

Second, courtesy our amazingly helpful embassy in Buenos Aires, I have learnt that Argentine agriculture—which is globally competitive, highly modernised and profitable—has significant lessons for India's stagnating agriculture sector. Argentine farmers have adopted the most modern agriculture practices, including 'direct seeding cultivation' that is reportedly far better for soil conservation and avoids ploughing operations, thereby saving on costs as well. Moreover, there is apparently an Argentine company called El Tejar that specialises in aggregating production from small and medium farmers, provides them with modern

technologies and inputs and thereby helps them to significantly raise their productivity and incomes.

These examples should be of immediate and direct interest to India, where a second green revolution is urgently needed if we are to achieve food security and avoid the emergence of political strife on the issue of food. Yet, my apprehension is that none of these relevant global practices will find their way into Indian agriculture as long as the government has the exclusive mandate for modernising the sector. Let us accept that agriculture today is far too important a sector to be left to the government.

For decades, the miserable state of our small and marginal farmers has been used as an excuse to direct increasingly large amounts of subsidies to the agriculture sector. These, as expected, do not reach the intended beneficiaries. The same argument has been used by Indian negotiators in the World Trade Organization (WTO) to demand additional safeguards against imports and ask for deeper cuts in the subsidies paid by advanced economies. While subsidies to giant agro-businesses in the US and Europe are a scandal, it is not clear how the safeguards that Indian negotiators get stuck on will help raise the productivity and income levels of small and marginal farmers.

Surely, we need well-directed and innovative policies—and not merely safeguards—to lift these millions of farmers out of this low-income trap. Instead, it is quite evident that the current nexus of misdirected subsidies, price support, import and export controls, collapse of extension services, absence of an agricultural land market and pervasive, corrupt bureaucratic intervention across the entire range of the rural economy will keep small and marginal farmers in a perpetual state of relative poverty for the foreseeable future. But this need not be so.

As the nearly three-decade-long dairy experience has shown, with private initiative and minimum official support, breakthroughs in dairy farming have made India the largest milk producer in the world. And just like in crop agriculture, dairy in India continues to be made up of very small producers, the great majority with only one or two milch cattle. This breakthrough was achieved by the National Dairy Development Board (commonly known as Mother Dairy) under the leadership of Verghese Kurien.

The same model can surely be applied to crop agriculture. A private operator such as El Tejar could be encouraged by some of our provincial governments to initiate such an aggregation process. It would start a cooperative or corporate process of renting land from a large number of small and marginal farmers, offering them higher incomes both as rents and as wage incomes. It would use the aggregated land to undertake agriculture with new techniques, rational use of inputs and benefit from the economies of scale and scope. This would help raise yields and achieve the breakthrough that can put Indian agriculture on a path of rising incomes and global competitiveness. The small and marginal farmer will be liberated from the destiny of poverty, and the back-breaking labour and dependence on corrupt officialdom that comes with it.

Is there another way forward that avoids private sector initiative and relies on a statist model to achieve such a breakthrough? I am certainly not aware of it and I invite feedback. Let us find an answer quickly because time is running out. We cannot continue relying on good monsoons and a patient poor peasantry that accepts being left behind. We need to think boldly and urgently to avoid a crisis in Indian agriculture whose economic, social and, indeed, political costs will surely be unaffordable.

16

Liberating the Farmer

THE surprisingly overwhelming response to my previous article (Farm Fresh from Argentina) has amply demonstrated that readers are acutely concerned about the state of our agriculture, because many see it as headed towards a real crisis. Some pointed at the archaic laws that govern land lease and sales and others at the continuing ban on inter-state movement of agricultural produce as major impediment to the modernisation of the sector, which are preventing it from benefiting from economies of scale and scope. These are surely valid issues. But the way to overcome these constraints is to facilitate the entry of private, cooperative or commercial investors in any segment of agriculture. These investors will generate the impulses to change the ground realities of archaic laws, the ban on inter-state movement, the tyranny of petty *babudom* or the dysfunctional working of the entire range of service providers who see their mandate not as providing a particular service but as a license for generating rents.

In my experience in villages around Delhi, one cannot hope to have an improved supply of electricity for the water pump by installing a captive step-up transformer or to get a 'crop loan' sanctioned or even a sale deed registered despite 'connections' and the 'computerisation' of land records, without paying a 'reasonable bribe'. To add insult to injury, there is simply zero concern among rent collectors about any accountability or fear of being apprehended. A clear distinction is maintained between the *de jure* and *de facto*, and you are constantly reminded that *de jure* is only *'dikhane ke vaste'* (for appearances only!). Try and follow rules, and you

get only grief. I am quite convinced that this malgovernance in rural India generates the widespread feeling of gross injustice that feeds the Naxalite and other forms of militancy, whose avowed goal is to overthrow such an exploitative state.

Can this chasm between *de jure* and *de facto* that has managed to choke off progress in agriculture be eliminated or minimised? The Naxal way out, though glamorous and romantic to some of our urban chic, is doomed to failure. Then, there are the well-meaning and sincere civil society organisations that are fighting heroic but localised battles. The hope is that these 'fireflies' will be connected and brought together to create a large enough impact. Unfortunately, I have not seen that happening. Perhaps Arun Maira, who coined the term fireflies, can connect them now that he is in a position to do so. Then, there are the microfinance guys who rely on social collateral and relatively high rates of interest to try and generate incomes and raise productivity. Yet even the largest of these, such as BRAC (then Bangladesh Rural Advancement Committee) and Grameen Bank in Bangladesh, whose efforts are praiseworthy, have so far apparently been unable to make a big dent on rural poverty and stagnation in agriculture.

These efforts do not appear to be a substitute for real commercialisation of agriculture and converting the 'peasant' into a viable, globally competitive farmer, whose self-interest in bringing in new technology and fresh investment coincides with that of fragmented landholders and rural wage earners.

If such commercialisation can be achieved in agriculture, the government's role will switch from being a supplier of services and inputs to regulation and supervision. This will be liberating and hugely productivity enhancing as experience in other sectors has shown. Civil society organisations will also be far more effective in ensuring that the government and large corporate entities do not collude and connive against the small landholders and wage earners as they will have a much more visible and larger target for their actions rather than the ubiquitous *babu* or the *patwari* against whom any opposition is but in vain.

So my suggestion is to start with the other end of the spectrum and encourage modern retail organisations and companies to establish direct supply links with farmers. The ideal will be to replicate the Coop experience in Scotland and parts of Europe where farmers have gotten together to achieve the desired direct connectivity to the market rather than work through layers of intermediaries.

It has been pointed out to me that the National Dairy Development Board (NDDB) experiment with organising small oilseed producers in Gujarat, on similar lines as dairy farmers, had failed. It would be useful to look at the reasons for that failure and draw the necessary lessons to make it work in the present conditions, which may be different. And we should also consider allowing and encouraging foreign multi-product retail companies to establish their agro-procurement operations for the Indian domestic and export markets. They could bring with them much needed investments in logistics, new technologies and the capacity to fend off the *babu*.

The small farmers' interests against those of large retailers can be protected by a vigilant civil society and a robust regulatory mechanism. This will liberate us from the situation where agriculture is starved of investment and new technologies, and wilts as a result of stifling and all-pervasive bureaucratic intervention.

17

Crying out for Speedy Reforms

AT a recent India-China book launch, where Human Resource Development Minister Kapil Sibal was present, I made it a point to highlight the comparative picture between India and China in the education sector. This is a crucial sector for emerging economies attempting to achieve inclusive and rapid growth. Moreover, as several recent studies have brought out, returns on skill formation and higher education, which are already substantial, continue to rise as the world increasingly takes on the attributes of a knowledge economy. By the way, the book by Mohan Guruswamy and Zorawar Daulet Singh titled 'Chasing the Dragon: Will India Catch up with China?' is well worth a read for all those interested in finding out the distance we have to cover to catch up with China.

India's adult literacy is 61 per cent compared with China's 91 per cent. Expenditure on education as a percentage of total public expenditure is 10.7 per cent and 12.8 per cent, respectively. China has 708 researchers per million population compared with 19 in India. In 1990, publications by Indians in journals were 50 per cent higher but in 2008, Chinese publications outnumbered Indian ones by 2:1. In 1985, the number of PhDs in science and engineering in India were 4,007 and 125 in China, but by 2004, China had 14,858 PhDs, while we had increased the number to only 6,318. In 2007, Indians filed 35,000 patents compared with 245,161 in China. China is set to overtake Japan as the second largest research & development (R&D) spender after the US in the next

two years. It allocated 1.34 per cent of its GDP in 2005 on R&D (which, incidentally, is well below 3.6 per cent in South Korea) while expenditure on R&D in India was barely 0.61 per cent in the same year. We have only 12,000 vocational training institutes to nearly 500,000 in China. More than 19 per cent of the youngsters in China opt for higher education, while only 11-12 per cent Indian students end up in colleges and universities.

The comparison with China in educational attainments and performance is not meant to once again lament over how China is far ahead of us. The comparison is made simply to drive home the need to understand that the education sector in India today needs the kind of focussed and urgent policy attention that trade and industry did in the late 1980s, which led to their reforms in 1991.

Education reforms and progress are the most important and critical policy issue in the country today. Otherwise, we may soon discover that our much-touted demographic dividend has remained an illusion and instead morphed into a disaster as large groups of unemployable youth, unable to join the workforce, end up swelling the ranks of extremists and insurgents. India will have to earn its demographic dividend and time is actually running out because the window is a relatively short one.

There is little to be achieved by tinkering at the edges, for example, by raising the bar for taking the IIT entrance examination or making the Xth standard exam voluntary. These are at best distractions. What is needed are bold and large-scale reforms that will shake up the sector and allow for new ideas, initiatives, and dynamic new organisations to take roots. We have to take the academic community along in implementing these reforms rather than have teachers at loggerheads with the government on issues of pay, autonomy or curriculum design.

The HRD minister is well aware of the need to think boldly, as is reflected in his statements prior to and after taking charge. The forthcoming Education Bill provides the opportunity to implement the required reforms. These would include: doing away with dysfunctional organisations such as UGC, AICTE, MCI and the other 13 professional councils at the national, and at the state level, which, as recent events have shown, are riddled with malpractices and vested interests; establishing multiple independent accreditation systems; allowing profit generating companies to enter this sector so that there is greater transparency in revenue generation; doing away with the plethora of controls, regulations and licences; expanding teachers' training and vocational training capacities manifold by both increasing public sector allocations and attracting private investment in these areas; creating an accessible and large commercial bank credit pool for education loans and massively expanding the number of scholarships to improve equity and access.

Fifty-four per cent of India's population is below the age of 25. We will add 150 million people to the workforce in the next 15 years and have a huge backlog to clear, with graduate unemployment running at nearly 20 per cent. The gross enrolment ratio for higher education, at present at 12 per cent, has to be raised to more than 40 per cent if the young population is to be converted into productive human capital. And Indians spend nearly $5 billion to educate their children abroad! This big domestic demand base can be used to convert India into a global education hub that attracts students from all over the world. This will contribute not only to our gross domestic product—in the US and the UK foreign students contribute $15 billion and $5 billion annually—but also build an India constituency. To achieve this, we need to look at higher education as a sector in which India has a big potential comparative advantage. But, for this to happen, the centre needs to think boldly, take action urgently and not get caught in a defensive, protectionist and controlling mindset.

18

Big Retail, Big Benefits

I do not normally write about or comment on the research output from ICRIER, the policy research think tank that I head, simply to avoid being accused of blowing one's own trumpet. I break this rule today only because the recent ICRIER report on the impact of the entry of large organised retailers on *kirana* stores, the consumers and farmers takes up an issue that directly affects all readers of this column. The feedback will be extremely useful in taking forward the policy recommendations made in the report. The study is based on the largest ever survey of *kirana* stores (2032), consumers (1,397), intermediaries (100) and farmers (197) ever undertaken to understand the ground realities of the Indian retail sector.

Some of the salient findings of the report are: i) the retail sector is likely to grow at least at 13 per cent annually; ii) at this rate, the value of retail trade will increase from $300 billion in 2005 to $590 billion in 2012; iii) the share of unorganised retailers who are likely to see their sales expand at 10 per cent annually will continue to remain a healthy 84 per cent of this expanded market; iv) however, the report emphasises that the growth of modern and large-scale retail is inevitable and indeed necessary to meet the growing demand as urbanisation picks up pace. Consequently, large retailers can expect to see an annual growth of nearly 40 per cent driving their share from 4 per cent in 2005 to 16 per cent in 2012. These findings highlight that the modernisation of the retail sector remains a positive sum game as the growing economy offers sufficient space for both segments to grow and thrive by exploiting their

specific strengths and USPs. The report should help douse some of the heavy emotion and rhetoric that has tried to portray the entry of large retailers as sounding the death knell of traditional *kirana* stores.

In fact, only a handful of *kirana* storeowners felt that they would have to exit the sector because of the entry of large companies. As many as 54 per cent felt that they will continue with the business and upgrade and modernise their facilities and 44 per cent even saw their next generation continuing with the family business. The report emphasises that the traditional *kirana* stores constitute an integral part of local community life and play a role beyond being the last unit of the supply chain. Consumers surveyed for the study mentioned their preference for a continued coexistence of both the local *kirana* store and the 'mall' as they met distinct consumer needs. Keeping this in mind, the report has focussed its policy recommendations on measures to nurture the unorganised retailers.

Some major recommendations are: i) increasing the access of unorganised retailers to commercial bank credit as only 12 per cent currently have such access and the remaining relied either on family capital or informal credit markets; ii) local governments should improve infrastructure for wet markets and local shopping centres as has been done in countries like China, Singapore and Malaysia; iii) the government should encourage corporatisation of unorganised retailers as has happened in the UK and Europe so that they benefit from modern logistics and procurement practices; and iv) the government should encourage large modern retailers to develop a self-regulatory code of conduct for their interaction with small producers, especially small and marginal farmers. This has to be reinforced by strengthening the role of the hitherto dormant Competition Commission to prevent collusion and predatory pricing behaviour.

One of the most important findings of the report is that farmers' profitability increases by as much as 60 per cent when they deal directly with large corporate retailers as compared to either intermediaries or selling their product in the local *mandi*. This represents a significant improvement in terms of trade for the farmer. Moreover, our survey reveals that given the complete collapse of the government-agriculture extension system, large retailers would emerge as the principal channel for taking new seeds, agriculture practices and technologies to the farmers. Thus, modern retail corporations could well emerge as the harbingers of the second green revolution. For this singularly important potential contribution alone, the government must consider removing all the remaining hurdles in the entry of large scale and modern retailers. The report points to the 30 plus clearances currently needed by a large corporation, either domestic or foreign, for entering into the sector. Moreover, these requirements are generally non-transparent and non-uniform across states. This situation needs to be rationalised so that modernisation of the Indian retail sector can proceed on required lines.

Modernisation of retail does not result in any loss of employment. The survey of the *kirana* stores shows that despite an initial decline in profitability (10 per cent) and turnover (8 per cent), small retailers actually employ more workers. Moreover, modern retail, we know, is also a labour-intensive activity. Any attempt to show retail sector modernisation as leading to loss of employment must be seen as spurious and against ground realities. Modernisation of the retail sector will contribute to inclusive growth and should therefore be encouraged.

19

Bold Vision Needed for Exports

THE new five-year foreign trade policy (FTP) will be announced on August 27, 2008. This is an opportunity for the Commerce and Industry minister, who has just signed two free trade agreements (FTA) (with South Korea and ASEAN) in less than 10 days, to reverse the plummeting trend in our exports and set the medium-term course for Indian exports to achieve a sustained and high-growth trajectory.

It is clear that with our exports stuck at around 1 per cent of global exports for the past 60 years, our policies have not been successful in making India an exporting nation. The external environment is clearly not the most propitious with world trade expected to decline by 9 per cent in 2009, the sharpest fall in more than two decades. It is, therefore, a formidable challenge to give exports a real push and needs a bold and innovative approach that must, however, also be fully cognisant of our ground realities.

As is, perhaps, well known, India's share has been stuck at around 1.3 per cent of global exports. It was so in 1991, when we undertook liberalisation and still is (2008). In contrast, China's share has increased from 1978, when their reforms started, till the end of 2008. Therefore, the first element in adopting a new approach would be to jettison the practice of expressing our export targets in absolute terms ($ billion) and instead state it in terms of raising India's share in global exports in the next 5 or 10 years. My own suggestion is to give ourselves an ambitious yet eminently achievable target of doubling our export share every 5 years.

That this can be achieved is shown by China having raised their exports of merchandise exports from $593,326 million in 2004 to $ 1,428,488 million in 2008.

To achieve this target, we will have to adopt a far more focussed approach to our export promotion measures and also shift from our current reliance on fiscal sops to actually attacking the structural impediments that, at present, shackle our exporting community. A simple exercise shows that the top 20 product categories account for 80 per cent of our total exports and 60 products account for almost 99 per cent. We must, therefore, ensure that our policy attention and export promotion measures are accordingly strongly biased in favour of these 20 product categories so that we can build a real global presence based on our revealed competitive advantage.

Similarly, it emerges that Asia's share in our total exports has risen from 22.5 per cent in January 2006 to 26.4 per cent in January 2009, the sharpest increase compared with any other region. The EU's share has also increased, though not as much. We have to, therefore, make sure that our promotion efforts in terms of regional offices, presence of commercial counsellors and so on is directed more to Asia and that we move purposively to finalise the FTA with the EU, which is already in the works. It is worrisome that the growth rate of our software exports, which was as high as 38 per cent in 2005-06, has been consistently slowing down in the past four years, even before the onset of the global crisis. It came down to less than 20 per cent in 2008-09 and is likely to be in single digits in 2009. As an innovation, the commerce minister, in consultation with his cabinet colleagues, will do well to include issues in growth of our remittances and tourism within the purview of the medium-term FTP.

Remittances and tourism are strongly and obviously labour intensive and also improve regional equity. Both the slowdown in software and other services exports, including tourism, and the virtual stagnation in the global share of our merchandise exports, requires that we make an urgent and determined effort to address critical supply-side constraints, which are the principal reason for our rather poor export performance. These include the inevitable infrastructure bottlenecks, especially power availability, access to adequate commercial credit for the small and medium exporter, ironically, skill shortages and the all-pervasive inspector *babu raj*. These are real problems and nothing will be gained by simply ignoring them on grounds that these are inherent in our democratic system and so nothing can be done about them. In this case, we might as well give up our attempts at formulating long-term policies for any sector.

To this list, we should add the relatively high level of transactions costs that exporters have to bear in complying with procedural requirements and securing fiscal and other benefits due to them. A recent survey of 400 exporting firms as a part of a study showed that up to 20 per cent of exporters do not avail of export incentives due to the hassles involved and more than 50 per cent admitted to having had to incur some expenditure to avail the benefits under various schemes. This calls for a thorough review of the export promotion schemes with a view to rationalising and simplifying them and making them sharply focussed.

This must be done in a time-bound manner and undertaken with no preconceptions but rather on the basis of the demonstrated efficacy of particular measures. We often tend to become self-congratulatory on

India's low level of dependence on external demand. This is self-defeating simply because a poor economy like ours, with such vast unemployed human resources, would surely benefit from expanding its share in global exports because these are employment intensive and have significant multiplier effects. It is time we finally gave up our export pessimism and used the positive global sentiment about India to our advantage.

Section III

India and the Global Economy

20

The Mother of all Bailouts

THESE are unprecedented times. The post-independence generation in India gets to experience its first real financial sector crisis and near meltdown. Thank the Lord that it is elsewhere where a trillion dollars is less than one-eighth of the GDP! This will hopefully add to its growing confidence by realising that 'they in the developed west' can also make mistakes, can falter and are not infallible.

The success of India's software and outsourcing industry had already seen economics professors in the US questioning the merits of liberal and open economies. Now, the US president is urging the Congress to pass a bill that would effectively nationalise large parts of the financial sector, having already taken into government care the world's largest insurance company by pumping in $85 billion of taxpayers' money. One wonders how financial sector puritans reconcile this with their stand on moral hazard, market-determined incentive structures and no financial institution ever being too large to cause systemic distress. Clearly all these mantras parroted by 'believers' of the financial sector's prowess to optimise across markets and achieve equilibrium must look outdated and even foolish.

But I suspect there will be some who will see this episode as yet another exception that would prove the rule that there is simply no role for government intervention or even careful regulation. They will continue to insist that financial sector whiz kids, armed with Excel sheets and technical models, should be allowed a free run for their money (literally

so!). These are the same people who called the earlier Asian financial sector crisis an exception and who have waited in vain for the Chinese banking sector to come crashing down because it did not follow the free financial sector nostrums. These financial sector theologians begin to sound increasingly like the Marxists who continued with their misplaced faith, despite Stalin and Pol Pot, on the grounds that these were exceptions to the general theory of dialectical and historical materialism. We know that history treats such dogmatists rather unkindly.

Others who are concerned with sustaining inclusive and rapid growth and with ensuring that the financial sector plays its due role in the development process would do well to draw some preliminary lessons from the unfolding events. The first lesson must be that trying to make economics into a science with its inviolate laws that are universally applicable is simply foolish and must be discouraged. Economics has been and will retain its Adam Smithian characteristic of being enmeshed with ethics on the one side and political philosophy on the other. This implies flexibility in approach to suit prevailing circumstances and the ability to find the second best solution where the first best, even when identified, will simply not work.

The second lesson specific to the financial sector would be to not surmise that the financial sector must necessarily be administratively controlled and not be allowed the freedom to innovate, compete and use market-based incentives as far as possible. A liberalised, market-based and effectively supervised and regulated financial sector has played a significant role in promoting and sustaining rapid growth. But its contribution to inclusiveness or equity is surely open to question. The third lesson must be to put greater attention on incentives (and not only through administrative dictates) that will direct the financial sector to contribute more meaningfully to inclusiveness as well.

We can now move on to the lessons India can draw from the financial crisis. The first would be to improve the quality of information that banks, capital market operators and other financial sector entities normally put out and which is available to regulatory agencies. Clearly, one of the major reasons for the ongoing US turmoil is that the Fed or the SEC (Securities and Exchange Commission) could not see the real quantum and nature of risk that had been piled on to the balance sheets of all these goliaths who then collapsed under their weight.

Second, the assumption that some entities, such as investment banks and hedge funds, should remain outside the regulatory regime must be discarded. Even if it is true, as has been argued, that these entities deal only with rich investors and not the general household savers and, therefore, do not need to be regulated or supervised, it is clear that their actions (greed in most cases) ultimately do create systemic distress. This affects one and all. To bring these entities under the regulatory regime would require a substantial strengthening and revamping of regulatory capacities. The sooner that can be done, the better!

The third lesson would be that, short of creating a single financial sector regulatory authority, there needs to be much more effective and real-time coordination between regulators dealing with different segments of the financial sector. The recommendation that a working group be established to examine the feasibility of a single financial sector regulatory authority in India should be implemented as soon as possible. Its mandate should include suggesting modalities for effective and real-time coordination among sector-specific regulators, if a single authority is not considered appropriate.

Finally, we must identify the weaknesses of credit rating agencies, including a possible conflict of interest situation. While there may be no straightforward answers, it is vital to make a beginning and generate real research, and not advocacy, as some government-financed groups tend to do, which can then inform public policy in this crucial area. Those who convert a crisis into a learning opportunity will deservedly move forward, while dogmas must and should fail.

21

Protectionism and Obama

BARACK Obama's election has been cheered across India and for many good reasons. Once again, the US has shown remarkable qualities of social and political regeneration and surprised all of us with the depth and breadth of its democratic traditions. By electing Obama with a clear majority of votes polled, the American people have given the US a fresh opportunity to regain its preeminent position in the world, which it has enjoyed since the middle of the last century.

An Obama administration, if it does live up to the campaign promise of being less unilateral and more consultative, can restore US political leadership in countering global terrorism and pushing back the obscurantist forces of fundamentalism. While these may well be the necessary conditions for giving a fresh lease of life to Pax Americana, the sufficient condition must surely be Obama's effective handling of the ongoing global financial meltdown and reinforcing the positive features of globalisation and giving it the much needed human face.

The President designate has moved quickly, as he must, to try and reverse the recessionary tide and bring the US economy back on the growth path. But the world will, of course, be watching with great interest his handling of the multilateral economic and trading regime and his commitment to globalisation. Any sign that he is wavering in his support to a liberal and open global economy, will dent the US image perhaps beyond repair. Neither the US nor indeed the rest of the world can afford

this sudden diminution of the US role in the global economy, as it is not clear if others are yet ready to take it on.

In India, there are genuine concerns that going by his past pronouncements on outsourcing and manufactured imports, an Obama administration has a strong possibility of turning protectionist. Hopefully, retrograde steps like restricting outward investment flows or outsourcing and reducing the number of service visas will be resisted from within by his own economic advisory team, comprising as it does, of people like Paul Volcker, Larry Summers and so on who have been strong votaries of globalisation.

The negative effect of such protectionist steps on our software and ITeS industry can be significant. Nearly 70 per cent of our software exports of close to $40 billion are destined for the US market and, of this, a hefty 40 per cent are used by the US financial firms that are now in deep trouble. It will be more pertinent for the Indian delegation to pursue this important issue with Obama's advisory team than to try and take a lead on restructuring the international financial architecture at the forthcoming G-20 meeting in Washington.

President designate Obama, while he can, of course, take the protectionist route, is unlikely to do so for several reasons. First, he appears to be strongly committed to reversing the decline in US's global prestige and leadership that has happened during the Bush presidency, especially over the last four years. He cannot hope to achieve this by leading the US away from globalisation and turning his back to US's long-standing commitment to free market for goods and services. This will seriously erode the legitimacy that Pax Americana enjoys at present. A protectionist move by the Obama presidency must surely imply the beginning of the end of the US economic hegemony in the world and accelerate the shift away from the Atlantic basin to Asia.

Second, US firms with overseas operations, especially in Asia, will for good reason, resist these moves as their competitiveness and indeed survival will be threatened. The loss of competitiveness and eventual shutting down of these firms will also result in job losses within the US.

Third, any unilateral protectionist moves by the US will raise the spectre of competitive tariff escalation by its trading partners, which will surely exacerbate the current crisis and make a worldwide depression that much more possible. There are more than enough people within the US academia, and hopefully also within the administration, who can hammer home the dangers inherent in such an approach and thus stop the Obama administration from going ahead in the protectionist direction.

Fourth and last, higher protection levels will imply ringing the death knell of the Doha Round and, effectively, also the near complete loss of World Trade Organization's credibility and indeed legitimacy. I doubt if any US president can precipitate such an eventuality. These factors will hopefully ensure that while there will be plenty of threats, and perhaps even some calls from voluntary export restraints from the incoming administration, these will not be carried forward to actual imposition of higher tariff or non-tariff walls by the US.

On the other side, this administration could rely much more on the traditional and admirable American strengths of product innovation, technology upgradation and higher productivity to provide the real thrust for pulling out the US economy from the recession into which it has unmistakably slipped. Obama has himself emphasised these during his campaign. He will find out very quickly that in this positive approach for handling the global economic downturn, India, with its dynamic entrepreneurs and large supply of technical professionals, has a lot to offer. A knowledge economy-based Indo-US partnership can not only be a win-win for the world's two largest democracies, but also have significant positive externalities for the rest of the world.

22

How to Beat the Downturn

THE government has done its bit to try and prevent the current downturn from becoming avoidably longer and deeper. Three measures, namely, fuel price reduction, further loosening of the monetary policy stance and the $6 billion fiscal stimulus package, were announced over the weekend. The timing clearly was determined by the electoral cycle, as these measures could not perhaps be announced with the electoral code of conduct in place.

If true, this raises an important issue. Some policy responses may be urgently needed to address future national emergencies even during the 'election period'. Therefore, the Election Commission (EC) should consider some flexibility in the code of conduct to prevent serious harm happening from not being able to take the necessary action because of the code of conduct. One condition could be that all major parties agree on the necessity of such measures and inform the EC. The market response to the government package has been mixed. The widely shared perception is that the package was big and bold enough to provide the needed thrust to domestic demand or help raise investment intentions. More measures might surely follow but it would have been better if the Centre had been bolder and demonstrated the strongest possible commitment to sustaining growth.

More importantly, these announcements have to be supplemented urgently with action on the ground that will ensure efficient and effective utilisation of these additional public resources. These actions could

include, as also stated by the deputy chairman of the Planning Commission, efforts to absorb the additional Rs.3 lakh crore that have been pumped into the system through the supplementary budget, which was passed in November; pushing ahead with the highway and power projects and infusing more life into the urban renewal mission and the Bharat Nirman Yojana. This requires focussed efforts that can be achieved if there is realisation that this is crisis time. Our system unfortunately does not respond in a 'business-as-usual' scenario.

It is fallacious to argue that just because the global economy is in a downturn, our exports must necessarily decline and we should attempt to depend entirely on domestic demand for stimulating growth and 'decouple' the Indian economy from global markets. This is almost akin to arguing that we should now be raising import tariffs to prevent cheap imports from benefiting our consumers and giving the domestic producers a run for their money. This should be resisted. With net exports contributing a negative (-) 6 per cent to Indian GDP growth between 2003-2008 and with Indian exports still at less than 1.5 per cent of total world exports, export pessimism is totally uncalled for. Instead, this is the opportunity to take the axe to complicated procedures that still impair our export effort and make the numerous export promotion councils earn their keep. A poor, labour-abundant economy must necessarily depend on exporting its skills, either embodied in manufactured goods or as services or labour movement across borders. India cannot hope to be entirely different.

But the more important issue at this stage is for the private and public corporate sector to rise to the challenge and play its due role in fighting the downturn. This has so far not been forthcoming in any noticeable manner. The auto and cement companies have been quick to pass on the 4 per cent cenvat reduction, but this has so far not been emulated by other industries. Domestic firms have had a terrific profitability run for the last seven-eight years. They can certainly afford a slight decline in their margins to try and boost demand. Therefore, the private sector should not only immediately pass on the cenvat reduction to the consumer but also reduce prices further and match the cenvat reduction by an equal amount of price reduction over and above that. This is their national duty at this time. More importantly, such a price reduction also makes strong commercial sense. Better to reduce margins now and maintain healthy 'top lines' than having to cut down production and lay off workers and still be unable to save the bottom lines from declining. It is time to shift to a total revenue maximising model instead of maximising profits.

Similarly, commercial banks, with an average return to equity at more than 14 per cent in 2006-07, can contemplate lowering interests more than the anaemic 1 per cent that some have announced. The average cost of deposit in India is stated to be about 6 per cent and the prime lending rate now is above 13 per cent. While there are many constraints and mandated lending requirements for commercial banks, the spread does remain relatively high. This is best reflected in the net income differential, which is at about 3 per cent for the Indian banking sector. This is substantially higher than for banks in developed economies, where it is typically below 1 per cent and also higher than Chinese banks, where this is about 2.5 per cent.

This spread must be brought down, thereby lowering the cost of capital for investors. Credit-to-GDP ratio remains woefully low in our country and the exclusion ratio, which reflects the unbanked population, remains very high.

Finally, small and medium enterprises that surely are the largest employers do not have reasonable access to commercial bank credit at internationally comparable rates. These weaknesses can be addressed by administrative measures and should not take long to implement. An ongoing downturn is a good time to focus attention on these critical issues.

23

Waiting for the Chinese Switch

Aconference on 'Global Financial and Economic Crisis: Impacts, Lessons, and Growth Rebalancing' held recently in Tokyo, generated a rich discussion. The three questions that expectedly dominated the proceedings were: first, whether the so-called 'green shoots of spring' herald the beginning of a full-fledged global economic recovery; second, if the recovery in advanced economies and the US will be a V, U or L-shaped one; and third, if China will succeed in switching its growth drivers from external demand to domestic consumption. On the India story, which I presented, the general agreement was that while the Indian economy was suffering a hiccup, induced by a combination of policy-tightening and external shock, its medium-term growth potential at 8-9 per cent remains in place.

The International Monetary Fund (IMF) effectively preempted any speculation on the first issue by releasing its latest forecast on April 22, the first afternoon of the Asian Development Bank Institute conference. The Fund revised its forecast downwards, for the fourth time since July 2008. These estimates show that the world economy will contract by 1.3 per cent in 2009. Advanced economies are expected to contract by a record (-)3.8 per cent and Asia's newly industrialising economies by 5.6 per cent.

Among the advanced economies, the worst sufferers are likely to be Japan and Germany, likely to see output shrink by 6.2 per cent and 5.5 per cent in 2009. The UK and the Euro area will see GDP decline by

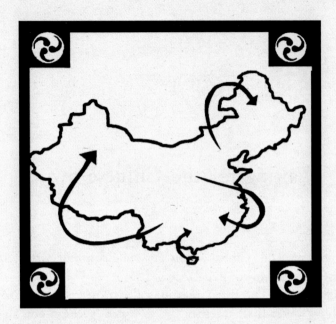

4.1 per cent and 4.2 per cent and the US by 2.8 per cent. The disturbing part of the forecast is that even in 2010, world output and advanced economies are not expected to achieve positive growth. Based on these somewhat chilling numbers, it can be said with some degree of confidence that the spring sprigs of recovery are a mere transient relief. We should cherish these, because the future perhaps has more disappointment and pain in store before recovery begins.

The IMF estimates that despite the massive fiscal stimulus, the US economy will decline by 2.8 per cent in 2009 and stagnate in 2010. Quite clearly, with the collapse of the financial sector and a loss of competitiveness in automobiles, consumer durables and electronics, the US economy is searching for new growth drivers. On the demand side, households that have suffered serious wealth loss and are faced with uncertain future employment and income prospects, are unlikely to raise consumption in the next couple of years. This brings to mind the prospects of the US following the experience of Japan's lost decade and an L-shaped recovery. So let us hope that the Obama administration's initiatives will yield early results. But it is difficult to see these take hold in less than two years. The best we can hope for is that Obama cans into his next campaign in 2011 with recovery having taken roots. Thus, we can at best expect a U-shaped recovery.

This implies that the world has to look for alternate sources of demand for at least the next 2-3 years. The recent strengthening of the dollar, of course, does not help. Let us hope that this trend will be reversed in the second-half of this year and the US will benefit from some additional external demand.

With the Euro area actually suffering a worse decline and likely to continue contracting in 2010, the only other major source of global demand is the Asia-Pacific region, where the growth impetus is largely dependent on China and India. IMF's forecast for the Indian economy for 2009 is 4.5 per cent. ICRIER has estimated Indian GDP to grow between 4.8-5.5 per cent in 2009-10, depending on the effectiveness of fiscal and monetary policy response. These estimates make the latest pronouncements of 6 per cent made by RBI and the Planning Commission to be on the optimistic side.

But the key question is whether the Chinese, with their $580 billion stimulus package, can successfully make the switch from external demand to domestic sources of growth. The paper at the conference by Bin Zhang and Yongding Yu argued that recent data pointed to the Chinese economy achieving a V-shaped recovery, with credit offtake, cement and steel production and manufacturing beginning to revive in March after the massive inventory correction of previous months. This is taken as evidence of the stimulus beginning to work and its multiplier estimated at 0.84 pushing up economic activity and employment in 2009 to achieve 6.5-7 per cent growth. But the two Chinese authors also correctly point to the acute need for significant structural reforms focussed on raising efficiency and productivity levels in non-tradable sectors for this recovery to be sustained and the switch from external to domestic demand being made successfully.

In this respect, both the Indian and Chinese economies are similar, in that future growth is dependent on successfully implementing the next generation of structural reforms. The world will watch with heightened anticipation the Chinese attempts at turning around the economic juggernaut and shoring up global demand. The Chinese miracle is best summed up by observing that in 1978, Deng Xiaoping had said that China could not do without global capitalism; three decades later, it is clear that global capitalism cannot do without China!

24

China's Investment Story

I write this from a freezing Beijing where I am ensconced in a well-heated deluxe room of the Lakeview Hotel at Peking University. The campus, which I had first visited in 1996, has been transformed since. It has reportedly received generous capital infusions of at least $100 million on several occasions during the last 15 years. I met a number of senior foreign academics who are attached to Peking and Tsinghua universities, whose infrastructure and quality of faculty are improving continuously. As an academic, I admit to feeling most envious of my Chinese counterparts.

But the real bonus of being here has been to find an answer to the question, how is China able to flood global markets with cheap exports without any evident infringement of WTO norms? The related issue is China's ability to push up investment levels to historically unprecedented levels. These investment levels have been used to expand the manufacturing base, and China has emerged as the second largest exporter after Germany. It is building up huge modern infrastructure capacities, which some would argue may be relatively overdeveloped, given China's current income levels. The simple answer, provided by Professor Michael Pettis, who is attached to Peking and Columbia universities, is that the Chinese have achieved this by effecting a massive and sustained cross-subsidisation of the productive/corporate sector by Chinese households. Chinese household savings have been transferred to the corporate sector through taxation, pricing and exchange rate mechanisms. These are

reflected in the consistently high corporate savings that are used for expanding capacities and for churning out low-cost tradable products. Real wages have been kept low and productivity growth has been kept at high levels, aided by a near-complete lack of industrial strife. The dismantling of 'iron bowl' practices in private and even state enterprises further encouraged high rates of household savings. Consequently, the share of wages in GDP has not risen. Savings were also encouraged by keeping the exchange rate undervalued, which effectively made non-tradable goods and services, which generally constitute a larger share of personal consumption in emerging economies, more expensive relative to tradable products. This promoted exports while restraining domestic consumption.

The flood of household savings, with recourse only to deposits in public sector banks, has been used to keep lending rates extremely low, thereby reducing the costs of capital for Chinese producers and exporters. For example, nominal interest costs have been kept at 6-7 per cent, when as a rule of thumb, Pettis argues, they should have been closer to the nominal rate of growth of GDP, which has been around 14-15 per cent.

Thus, Chinese exporters not only enjoyed an endless supply of cheap and highly productive labour, whose skills are being constantly upgraded, but they also enjoyed relatively low capital costs. Add to this the subsidy inherent in the availability of government-acquired land, abundant energy supplies, negligible environment and transactions costs, and we have a clearer picture of China's export competitiveness. This also implies, however, that Chinese producers, perhaps, have a negative value-added on the basis of domestic resource cost calculations. Has this been the story in other East Asian economies during their own periods of high growth and export orientation? Perhaps, but not for long, as both Japan and Korea were restrained after a point by strong external pressures. But China took the extra step of accumulating US treasury bills at levels never seen before and bought itself an insurance policy against US intervention.

Can this continue? Not indefinitely, for sure. Ignoring external pressures, which will inevitably emerge domestically as well, China cannot sustain this for too long. As another panellist, Professor Xu Xinzhong, argued, the low level of consumption may not be due to the share of wages in GDP remaining low, but it may be due to the growing income and regional inequalities that exclude an increasing number of people from the benefits of rapid growth. This is already generating unsustainable social stress and pressures to put in place a social security system and to protect the environment from deteriorating further. Farmers are also beginning to protest against the government's acquisition of land which, so far, has been routinely handed over to industrial enterprises. Further, the renminbi (¥) had been allowed to appreciate for two years prior to the onset of the current global crisis, reducing to some extent the price distortion between the non-tradable and tradable sectors. However, the renminbi has again been pegged to the dollar ($) since July, when the latter started depreciating against major currencies. A large part of the Chinese fiscal stimulus has also been directed at creating infrastructure capacities instead of pushing up household consumption. Thus China, along with the US, may successfully shift the cost of adjusting the global macroeconomic imbalances to the rest of the world. The US could well go along as it helps its own recovery if China continues to finance its deficits. The US stance will become clear during US President Barack Obama's visit this week.

Section IV

India and Global Governance

25

Challenges Ahead for G-20

THE second G-20 summit in London has generated high expectations from a world that is becoming increasingly anxious about the length and depth of the ongoing global recession. The mood in Europe, where I was last week, and in North America is deeply sombre as people expect the economic news to get worse before it gets better. The nightmare scenario is of the US remaining trapped in a Japan-like L-shaped recovery that engenders a prolonged recession and rising unemployment in OECD economies and a sharp slowdown in emerging economies. This could trigger competitive protectionism, which, if it comes to pass, would surely see the world economy plunging into a depression. Therefore, the immediate and most urgent challenge before the leaders in London is to prevent such a nightmare scenario from being played out.

The necessary condition for meeting this challenge is to recognise that it is dangerous at this time to pursue narrowly defined national interests. Instead, the G-20, acting cooperatively, has to forge a global agenda for pulling the world back from the edge of the chasm of depression.

For the G-20 to achieve a common objective and purpose, two institutional advances are required. First, that the grouping should now be given a formal status. At present, even the composition of the G-20 is fluid with members and invitees being added virtually at the discretion of the host country. This neither inspires confidence nor lends credibility to the formation.

Second, there still exist sub-groups within the G-20, which meet at the sidelines and come up with their own mini-*communiqués* and declarations. This fosters the 'us and them' environment that is surely not conducive to collective resolve and action. So, the G-20 member countries should agree to give up their membership of other groupings. One of the more important implications of this move will be the disbanding of G-7, which is seen as an anachronism both in European and American academic circles. Let us hope that G-7 leaders will announce in London that the next meeting in Italy will be its last. This will be the needed unambiguous signal from developed economies that they are serious about expanding the high table for global governance.

The leaders will do well to focus principally on setting the global financial house in order by agreeing to some concrete actions with a time-bound plan for implementation. This is the root cause of the present economic distress and any future global economic recovery is critically premised upon restoring the financial sector back to normalcy. This will require that the leaders to agree to implement some immediate measures to unfreeze the financial markets and get credit moving again.

Some of the actions that can be agreed to are: first, to bring all financial agents under some form of national regulatory oversight that is comprehensive in nature. This will eliminate the 'shadow financial sector', which, because of its extraordinarily high leverage ratios and transactional opacity, was at the root of the recent financial sector meltdown.

Second, there has to be an agreement that given the huge complexity and heterogeneity of financial systems and of financial transactions across countries, a global financial super regulator is simply not feasible. Nicolas Sarkozy, having apparently been advised by Joseph Stiglitz, feels strongly on this issue. But he should recognise that such an insistence will, at this stage, only distract from the main task at hand and generate dissonance when least required. I hope there will be agreement on national regulation on the basis of some universally agreed standards and norms, which is the practical solution at this time.

Third, the leaders should agree that the present regulatory regime that assures a 'level playing field' in the financial sector needs to be replaced with a regulation that creates a set of incentives that lead to risk being allocated to where there is a risk-bearing capacity. For instance, institutions with a capacity for diversifying risks across time, would not have to put aside reserves/capital/margins for illiquid assets, while institutions without long-term funding or liabilities would have to.

Finally, it will look too much like 'business-as-usual' if the only tangible decision emerging from the London Summit is to increase the IMF capital base to $500 billion without any reform of the institution, which was being seen as redundant and was downsizing its staff less than a year ago. Therefore, it should be agreed that the IMF must be reformed before its capital base is further enlarged.

These reforms would include getting some visible distance between the IMF and the treasuries of some OECD economies and making it a more broad-based institution, both in terms of selecting its top management and the professionals who work there. These two steps will make the IMF a more representative, legitimate and credible organisation. The move to enlarging the voice and representation of emerging economies should not await the change in IMF quotas. Instead, a system can be designed on the lines of the WTO where major countries come together informally to discuss the major issues and then take their consensus to the broader membership. A criteria which includes both the country's share in the global economy/trade and its share in the global population, may be used to determine its quota in the IMF. This alone may provide the basis for achieving a desirable 'voice and representation' structure.

26

Dragon Conquers G-20 Summit

THE London Summit of the G-20, attended by leaders representing over 85 per cent of the world's economy and population, agreed to a 29-point *communiqué*, which, as is common with such declarations, pushes all the buttons and is drafted expertly to provide a rousing call for ushering in global recovery. This has brought much needed cheer to markets across the world.

However, the *communiqué* also reflects an exercise in compromises to keep everyone on board. The US did not get the explicit commitment for each country making its fiscal stimulus at a minimum of 2 per cent of GDP. On the other side, the Europeans, especially the French, coached by American economist Joseph Stiglitz, did not get a supra global regulator for the financial sector.

But there are two clear winners—China and the IMF. The *communiqué* is silent on global imbalances and exchange rate misalignments. These are seen by some to be, along with the monumental regulatory mistakes in the financial sector, the fundamental causes of the present crisis. The Chinese will also be happy at the possibility of a Chinese heading either of the two Bretton Woods institutions, the next time round.

The London Summit, in that sense, can be seen as a rite of transition for China to emerge as a major player in the global scene. The Chinese media has gone to great lengths to show the US and China working

together to help achieve common ground and bring about convergence. The London Summit has been, thus, about the emergence of the G-2—the new power relationship between the US and China—which will be the most influential factor in global issues in times to come. This reflects ground realities as well. For, a successful recovery from the current recession is contingent upon the US and China meeting their respective challenges successfully. The unfreezing of credit flows in the US will happen only when all toxic assets in its banking system have been fully identified and taken off from the banks' balance sheets. This is at the heart of the recently announced Tim Geithner plan (toxic assets). Second, the unprecedented slowdown in US consumption demand has to be compensated by a similar rise in domestic demand in China. This will allow the Chinese to switch their production capacities to cater to domestic demand. The success of these plans is far from guaranteed. Can the US banks fully identify their toxic assets when these continue to rise either because of housing foreclosures or the worsening state of consumer credit? Moreover, the Geithner plan could well flounder in its attempt to use private bidders for making the price discovery for toxic assets.

China's effort to switch production to meet domestic demand may run into problems related to the required absorptive capacities at the level of its provinces and counties, who have so far encouraged savings. Moreover, the transaction costs of supplying to domestic markets can be significantly higher than servicing foreign export markets. Thus, China could find it difficult to achieve a seamless transition from the extreme export-orientation to domestic demand-led growth. The rest of the world would do well to figure out the fall-back options in case one or both of these challenges prove more intractable than envisaged.

Apart from the emergence of the G-2, the other tangible result from the London Summit has been the phoenix-like rise of the IMF. This has happened through a trebling of its resources to $750 billion and the *communiqué* stating that it will be responsible, along with the Financial Stability Board (FSB), for developing an early warning system and as a provider of emergency financing for beleaguered economies. It was not long ago that the principle task of the then newly-appointed IMF managing director was to prune staff and somehow keep it afloat financially. But it is not clear how the Fund has restructured its capacities and redesigned its diagnostic tools for it to play a more effective role, than in the past, in pulling individual economies out of the crisis. I have not so far seen any evidence of the Fund having drawn some lessons from the current crisis. Throwing money at the crisis may be a necessary but certainly not a sufficient condition for engendering a sustained recovery.

This has, perhaps, been the greatest weakness of the G-20 process. The leaders, for reasons best known to them, have chosen not to ask for a complete overhaul or restructuring of existing institutions or given them new mandates or fresh instruments with which to tackle the challenges ahead. This surely implies that we will continue to treat the present crisis, and others to follow, simply as a repetition of past episodes and, therefore, apply the same worn out methods to handle them.

One would have thought that a crisis of this magnitude at the very centre of global capitalism would have goaded the leaders to look for fresh ideas and insights. Instead, we ended up with three times the old wine in the same old bottles. The beltway bureaucracies, whom Obama professes to fight, win yet again!

27

Contours of Global Governance

IT was a learning experience to have participated in two international conferences that focussed on issues on the agenda of the 2009 G-20 Summit in Pittsburgh. The first, called the Global Economic Symposium, was organised by the Institute of World Economics, Kiel, Germany. The second was an international conference in Delhi, organised by ICRIER in collaboration with two premier European think tanks, Centre d'Etudes Prospectives et d'Informations Internationales (CEPII) in Paris and Bruegel in Brussels. The Delhi conference (September 14-15) brought together participants from 15 of the G-20 countries. This reflects widespread interest among both advanced and emerging economies, especially in trying to distil lessons from the global financial and economic crisis and taking forward the agenda on financial sector reforms, preventing incipient and murky protectionism from taking hold and discussing the possible contours of global governance in a multipolar world. The remark by former Reserve Bank of India governor that the G-20 agenda is in danger of being hijacked by the US and the UK adds urgency and importance to these efforts at bringing together academics and researchers from both advanced and emerging economies. Both conferences highlighted the importance of developing well-researched and well thought-out positions that can be used to drive the G-20 agenda in the right direction and ensure that emerging economies' interests are taken fully on board.

We, in India, need complete clarity on whether or not a proactive participation in informal groups such as G-20 or G-8 plus O5 (Outreach 5—emerging countries: Brazil, China, India, Mexico and South Africa) reconciles with our national interest. The question arises because many among us would tend to argue that given our limited share in global gross domestic product and trade (about 2 per cent and 1.5 per cent, respectively) and the relatively insulated and 'over-regulated' state of our commercial banking and financial system, we are not really affected by the global cycles and events.

Those who hold this view also argue that it is far more important for India to focus its limited governance capacity on addressing domestic supply-side constraints to achieve the potential growth rate, which is a necessary condition not only for fighting poverty but also for improving our standing in the global community and multilateral institutions. This view has some merit, as it basically advocates getting on with the national domestic reform agenda, achieve our growth potential and await our turn in the global governance stakes.

The alternate view is that India should seize the opportunity, at a time when G-8 countries are keen on its active involvement, to build a stronger case for its eventual membership of the UN Security Council, which remains a national aspiration. A more visible and proactive role in informal global groupings such as G-20, it is argued, will yield economic and security dividends in line with our long-term national interests, such as minimising the chances of losing a vote in multilateral institutions on making public a sanitised version of the India country strategy that mentioned a project in Arunachal Pradesh. A more prominent international stature will be more in line with our dynamic and evolving status in the global economic and strategic arena, a trend that was emphasised in both conferences.

Ascribing to the earlier view, I had argued for India to effectively disengage from these informal groups or simply to tread water and basically attend as an observer, awaiting its turn. But the discussion persuaded me to change my stance. It is amply clear that we cannot simply walk away from the expectations that our partners have of us. This will be akin to turning away from our global responsibilities and not be seen as worthy of an aspiring global player.

So, we have to remain engaged. And, therefore, the unanimous view was that emerging economy leaders, attending the G-20 meetings, should be better armed with inputs from think tanks working together and providing analysis and insights on issues. A network of G-20 think tanks and institutes needs to be built so that civil society and intellectuals can better influence the direction and substance of the ongoing transition in global governance.

There are, however, clear budgetary constraints for a revenue-strapped country like ours. But, the effort is well worth it and the return on resources allocated by the government on this research and networking will more than justify the outlay. Our Chinese counterparts have clearly shown the way by allocating some of their best human resources and large-scale financing to issues in global governance such as the adoption of an alternate reserve currency. Surely, India's richer friends will also not hesitate to lend a hand in mobilising such resources, provided there is a clear signal from the government about its interest in developing such capacities and networking. The Indian government can take the lead by establishing a mixed working group comprising government and academics to provide inputs for those participating in the summits or its preparatory meetings. Such broad-based interaction can prevent the agenda from being hijacked by any interest group and also, as the lecture by Professor Andrew Sheng at the Delhi conference highlighted, prevent a consensus emerging simply by default.

28

Tangible Results of Pittsburgh

THE Pittsburgh Summit has clearly pronounced that, 'Today, we designated the G-20 as the premier forum for our international economic cooperation.' This should normally imply the demise of G-8, which has so far been the premier informal forum for global governance. It seems, however, that G-8 will continue to function, *albeit* economic issues may be formally off its agenda, which could henceforth be more focussed on geostrategic and political issues. This will result in a two-track global governance architecture, which, in my view, does not really work. With a smaller number of richer and more powerful members, G-8 will continue to be seen as the real power centre or the 'high table of global governance'. One cannot see any hosting country being able to prevent another G-8 member from bringing up a burning economic or financial problem during a G-8 summit. Therefore, the 'us and them' divide between advanced and dynamic emerging economies on the one hand and advanced economies on the other, will persist and this will not make for real and effective coordination.

The US seems quite prepared to replace G-8 with G-20. The real resistance, I am told, comes from relatively smaller powers such as the UK, Canada and Japan, who visualise a dilution of their global stature as a consequence. Perhaps, it will take time before the recognition sets in that a larger forum for global governance is more reflective of the present multipolar world and will be more effective in preventing any unilateral behaviour in future.

The second major announcement concerns the role and management of the IMF. The context for this changed role is to be provided by the 'Framework for Strong, Sustainable and Balanced Growth', which was launched at Pittsburgh and which visualises putting in place '…a process whereby we set out our objectives, put forward policies to achieve these objectives, and together assess our progress.' This is indeed revolutionary, because it implies that the biggest and most advanced economies will be required to ensure that their macroeconomic policies do not simply serve their national goals but are designed to take into account the externalities that these generate for the global economy. The IMF has been asked to undertake a '… candid, evenhanded, and balanced analysis of our policies,' and develop a '… forward looking analysis of whether policies pursued by individual G-20 countries are collectively consistent with more sustainable and balanced trajectories for the global economy.' The IMF will need to build on the existing surveillance mechanism and be truly neutral, unbiased and, most importantly, sufficiently competent technically to be able to analyse the risks inherent in national policies and assess their overall impact on other economies operating in an increasingly integrated global economy.

The Fund's past record in this regard has been somewhat weak. It has on various occasions either been unable to see a looming crisis (as in its Article IV consultations quite often presenting an outcome, which has been quite at odds from unfolding realities subsequently) or has pulled its punches to avoid ruffling feathers in national capitals. Partly though, this has been a consequence of hypersensitivity on the part of member countries to any critical evaluation of their policies. This is especially true of both the advanced and larger emerging economies.

The marked bias in the selection of staff in favour of a particular kind of economic and quantitative skills has also tended to sustain dogmas and succumb to 'one-size-fits-all' approaches. All G-20 members will have to accept some surrender of economic and financial sovereignty to the IMF and the newly broadened and more empowered FSB if the Fund has to effectively discharge its additional responsibilities.

One of the decisions from the Summit is to shift at least 5 per cent of quota share in the IMF to more dynamic emerging markets and developing countries from over-represented countries 'using the current quota formula as the basis to work from.' Given that the present quota formula principally relies on the country's share in global output and trade, it is not clear how this shift will be brought about except for China and a couple of advanced economies.

One of the suggestions at the pre-Pittsburgh Washington meeting was to also include population as one of the criteria for quota reallocation to facilitate this shift. The Summit has also called upon '… our Finance Ministers and Central Bank Governors to launch the new Framework by November by initiating a cooperative process of mutual assessments of our policy frameworks and the implications…for the pattern and sustainability of global growth.'

India and other large emerging economies will have to develop the capacity for participating in this mutual assessment of national policies and global trends so as to be able to analyse their impact on their own economic prospects. In our case, this may be best achieved by setting up a joint working group of the Ministry of Finance and the Reserve Bank of India that can undertake, with needed inputs from outside experts, an assessment of evolving global economic conditions and their impact on the economy. Creating such a capacity should be seen as the necessary condition for effective future participation in the G-20 process and for possibly hosting the summit in 2012 after Canada, Korea and France, which have already been identified as the next three hosts.

29

India and the WTO

Rethink Needed

THE future of the Doha Development Round (DDR) and strengthening the multilateral trading regime (MTR) in the context of rising protectionist sentiments globally should be the top priorities for the incoming Commerce Minister. DDR has been in a state of suspended animation since December and it will be useful to resuscitate the Round before it goes beyond intensive care. The Minister should ask for an evaluation of the costs of 'no deal', and for a precise definition of a 'bad deal' for India, given our national interests. Before he gets bogged down in details, key in such negotiations, he would do well to formulate his broad view on whether a strong MTR is in India's national interests especially in the context of the leadership role India sees for itself in the evolving global governance. This, in my view, will most likely induce him to adopt a positive and more proactive stance for a successful conclusion of the DDR within a year of assuming office. Armed with this declared stance, he could put the onus on President Obama to secure the fast-track negotiating authority from the US Congress and for the US Trade Representative (USTR) to conclude his review of the present state as quickly as possible and return to the negotiating rooms.

I have noticed, ever since our 'great victory at Cancun', a degree of self-congratulation and satisfaction at thwarting a negotiated outcome. This was necessary then, seven years ago, but does this serve our interests

today? The disturbing feature has been that a section of our political leadership, academia and of course the sensation seeking media, has engendered an environment in which any negotiated outcome in the WTO is made out to be a 'political defeat' of the emerging economies, represented by India and Brazil, at the hands of those rich countries which use the WTO to exploit us. Surely that is *passé*!

It is time that this perception, that the WTO and the regime it oversees exclusively serves the rich countries' interests, is given up. The huge increase in WTO membership and the rising share of emerging economies in world trade shows this is not true. The world is not about 'us and them' any longer because globalisation has now firmly integrated our economies in the world trading and technology flows. It is clear that the credibility, legitimacy and ability of the WTO to enforce its decisions in dispute settlement cases will surely take a knock if DDR is abandoned. As a member of the Quad, India has a responsibility to ensure that WTO does not suffer this fate. So we should either opt out of the Quad on the basis that saving the DDR or the WTO is not in our interests at this stage or be ready to make acceptable compromises. At least we have to make sure that we are successful in projecting the correct picture that it is not India but others who stand in the way of a negotiated deal.

Nobody argues that we are better off with a more robust and liberal MTR rather than having to negotiate a plethora of bilateral and regional free trade agreements. Every bilateral negotiation has the danger of being captured by narrow sectional domestic interests and is excruciatingly slow makes the trading regime exponentially murkier and difficult to manage.

Let us briefly examine, given the space constraint, the likely impact on our sector interests, of a possible DDR deal as it was close to finalisation in July 2008. For sectors covered under the Non-Agricultural Market Access (NAMA), there would be a lowering of bound tariffs (and the US should simply drop its completely unreasonable demand of discussing only on the basis of applied rates) to about 15 per cent under the agreed Swiss formula with its coefficients. Our average applied rates are already lower and sectors, like auto, where applied rates are higher, will be protected under the special products dispensation. In return, we will achieve the reduction in peak tariffs in advanced country markets for our important exports like textiles and leather to below 7 per cent instead of the 30 per cent or so they face today. Clearly, this serves our national interest.

In the services sector, we have a comparative and competitive advantage and need to liberalise sectors like legal services, accountancy and media to exploit their full potential. In financial services, the situation is unclear, given the crisis, and surely advanced economies, busy nationalising their banks, will not be making heavy demands. So here too I cannot see our national interests being compromised.

Finally we come to the agriculture sector. Agriculture and farmers have a right to benefit from the gains from international trade and be freed from the heavy hand of government intervention. I give three brief arguments in support of concluding the agriculture negotiations. First, reductions in export subsidies, domestic support and import tariffs in this Round can be seen as the first step to make agriculture more open and globally traded. This requires building of trust and assuring domestic groups that vital interests of food security are not being compromised. Second, our small and marginal farmers will not be deluged by subsidised imports because the great majority will be protected under the special safeguards mechanism that will allow about 7 per cent of agriculture tariff lines to be exempt from the agreed tariff cuts. And in any case, members are entitled to impose higher duties in case of import surges. There is then no question of our 'poor farmers' having to compete against the US treasury or the European bourses. Third, the plight of our small and medium farmers, as Ashok Gulati and Anwarul Hoda have brought out in their recent volume 'WTO Negotiations on Agriculture and Developing Countries' (2008), has much more to do with our own domestic policy generated constraints than the global trading regime. By negotiating agriculture, Mr. Sharma wills the agriculture ministry to implement the necessary reforms. Our farmers suffer more from lack of adequate electricity and new seeds and poor access to bank credit and markets than from subsidised import surges.

Given the above, I suggest that India should ask for a ministerial meeting to be convened as quickly as possible and put the onus squarely on others for dragging their feet. And for those who argue that DDR is past its 'use by date' and should be replaced by a more ambitious round of negotiations that includes climate change *et al,* I wish a greater degree of realism and hope that they recognise the importance of following a sequential approach, specially when we are in the midst of a transition in global governance.

30

Pumping New Life into Doha Round

DESPITE exhortations from successive G-20 summits, the Doha Development Round (DDR) has been in a state of suspended animation since July 2008. It is fortunate that protectionist measures taken by several governments since November 2008 have not resulted in a rash of competitive protectionism. But we are at the top of a very slippery path. It will not take much for governments to succumb to domestic protectionist pressures if unemployment continues to rise or the recovery falters. Therefore, it is quite important that the multilateral trading regime be strengthened and the credibility of the World Trade Organization (WTO), which serves as its global watchman, is enhanced. There can be no better means of achieving this than by ensuring a successful conclusion of the Doha Round.

In this context, it is sad to realise that a successful outcome of the Doha Round is seen as an increasingly remote possibility. There is talk of 'multilaterlising regionalism' which, in all honesty, is somewhat of an oxymoron. And some observers, on grounds of realism, have suggested that we accept a failed round as a *fait accompli* and start looking at the second best options. India and other emerging economies should not accept such a pessimistic prognosis. Instead, they need to ensure that the Doha Round is successfully concluded, even if with a lower ambition level.

In this context, the Indian initiative to hold a mini-ministerial conference in Delhi (on September 4-5) is indeed welcome. It is also heartening to note that most major WTO members and less developed countries have agreed to send their trade ministers as this will ensure that participation in this purely informal get-together would be seen to be fully representative of WTO membership.

This is vital, as in the absence of such a broad-based representation, the mini-ministerial could well be criticised as being exclusionary in nature and focussing only on issues of interest to a few advanced and large emerging economies. Henceforth, negotiating modalities in WTO should be such that all 150 members feel included and the process is seen as transparent and not one in which deals are reached behind closed doors by a handful of members. This will require that members of the so-called New Quad (the US, the EU, India and Brazil, with the latter two replacing Japan and Canada) have a far more active communications stance with the rest of the membership.

Moreover, formation of 'issue-based negotiating groups', which could reflect fluid negotiating geometries and coalitions, should be actively encouraged. The mini-ministerial would do well to focus principally on these 'process issues' to facilitate further progress. With an enlarged membership, likely to expand even further, modalities have to be agreed upon to ensure that outcomes and also the negotiating processes are inclusionary, equitable and transparent.

The most important change that has happened in WTO since the end of the Uruguay Round is the emergence of 3 or 4 large emerging economies such as Brazil, China, India and South Africa, which have had to be included among the small core group of negotiators. The emergence of the New Quad marks a major transition in global trade negotiating architecture and necessitates building up of trust and confidence among its members. The best means to build this trust is to try and achieve some collective success on issues that may require less compromise for all concerned. This would also lend support to accepting a less ambitious outcome if that is what is needed for the successful conclusion of the Doha Round.

The other transition being tackled in the Round is to bring agriculture within the ambit of the multilateral trade regime from which it has so far remained excluded. This is a historical undertaking, much more strategic in its implications than was, for example, the inclusion of textiles and the winding up of the multifibre agreement. This also took very long and required tremendous efforts and compromises. Agriculture is seen as a strategic sector in the context of food security. This gives extraordinary and disproportionate clout to domestic agriculture lobbies that have been hitherto successful in thwarting any move toward agriculture under the WTO discipline. A necessary condition for achieving this would be for WTO members to agree to an international convention on food security that would essentially disallow food being used as a strategic weapon against any other member country. This would also include protocols outlawing export restrictions and permitting action against cartels by an empowered WTO. The mini-ministerial conference could discuss holding such a global convention under the UN aegis.

In the meantime, we may agree to move forward on the basis of the understanding that was reached in July 2008. At that time, Indian negotiators were successful, having overcome strong resistance, in securing sufficient safeguards against import surges that could affect the livelihood of small and marginal farmers. A successful Doha Round that yields bound tariffs in NAMA (Non-Agricultural Market Access) which are above the present applied rates; protects our small and marginal farmers; and gives us greater market access for our competitive services exports would be entirely in India's interests.

By calling for the mini-ministerial, the Commerce Minister has already signalled India's intention to remain actively engaged. Now he only has to mobilise the political support within his party for concluding the Round. This must be his next priority!

31

Are we Isolated on Climate Change?

ABOUT a month ago, at a closed-door session on 'India and Global Climate Change', the main presenter, a former environment secretary, eloquently outlined the tough stand that India should adopt in partnership with China and Brazil in the forthcoming Copenhagen Summit. That this is the standard party line was clearly demonstrated by Union Environment Minister Jairam Ramesh in his recent dialogue with Hillary Clinton. India will not consider any capping of emissions by emerging economies and, in any case, advanced economies should demonstrate their seriousness by making substantial upfront funding (hundreds of billions of dollars) commitments for any meaningful advance to be made.

At this session (June 27), I had raised a somewhat practical question about what would India's position be in case the Chinese had a deal with the Americans. None of us had any inkling of what was brewing and exactly a month later (July 28) in Washington it transpired China and the US signed a memorandum of understanding (MoU) on enhancing bilateral cooperation on climate change, energy and environment. Unarmed with this information, the key presenter at the seminar asserted that the Chinese would never let India down and would not have any agreement with the US. Apparently, our minister subsequently accepted the explanation given by the Chinese ambassador that the MoU does not and will not lead to any bilateral understanding between China and the US in Copenhagen.

There are no complaints about the Chinese signing an MoU with the US, which is clearly in their national interest, given the high level of mutual economic and financial interdependence between the two nations. But one is amazed at India's apparent naivete in continuing to believe that when push comes to shove (and we can expect that the Obama administration, having already taken several domestic policy steps, will exert maximum pressure to secure an ambitious outcome at Copenhagen), we will not be left in splendid isolation. This happened to us in the last stages of the Uruguay Round (trade talks). It would appear that the great majority of countries feel that a consensus and globally coordinated action on climate change is necessary. Therefore, our prime minister did well to sign the joint statement in L'Aquila, despite the naysayers. He surely understands that to remain in the game, we have to be seen as a cooperative player.

One wonders how policymakers will act, now that the details of the Sino-US MoU are out. The MoU clearly states that 'The purpose is to strengthen and coordinate our respective efforts to combat global climate change and support environmentally sustainable and low-carbon economic growth.' It adds that, 'The participants intend to hold regular ministerial consultations to deepen mutual understanding and promote and guide bilateral cooperation on climate change.' Two questions arise: First, will we continue to formulate our stance on the assumption that the Chinese will support us when the going gets tough, and is there any mileage in that support if they are regularly consulting with their US counterparts? Second, how come the Chinese are able to pull off such a publicity coup despite their stated opposition to the US? They have signed an MoU that is long on bilateral cooperation, yet gives them sufficient freedom in the ongoing negotiations.

A part of the answer to this question came forth in a recent interaction with senior Chinese counterparts who said that Indian negotiators were so good that once they had spoken either at WTO or UNFCCC, there was nothing left for the Chinese delegates to say! How one wished this role was reversed in the future. The validity of India's argument against accepting emission caps, which is based on our low per capita levels and the undertaking to keep it lower than advanced economies has also been recently challenged.

In a Wall Street Journal article (July 23) the managing director of Brookings, William J. Antholis, has questioned the credibility of this stand. He argues that by adding over a billion people by 2050, China and India will undermine the '...Careful consensus (on population management) developed over a decade ago, with India's support, at the 1994 United Nations International Conference on Population and Development.' Antholis adds that on this basis '... countries like India are using a double standard when they talk about history. ... If developed nations are held responsible for emissions that they historically contributed, oblivious to their impact on climate change, why shouldn't developing nations take responsibility for producing generations of people who will generate emissions into the future?' It is clear that advanced economies will not accept the proposition that historical behaviour obliges them to accept completely asymmetric unilateral action for mitigation. The issue clearly is that somehow a workable modality has to be found for all nations to work together to prevent an unacceptable outcome. In this context, is there a way forward in which India could again regain the high ground and not lose the narrative? Some pointers for a credible stand for India have been provided by Nobel laureates Thomas Schelling in a recent lecture and Michael Spence, in his paper titled 'Climate Change, Mitigation and Developing Country Growth'.

Closer home, Ramgopal Agarwala has produced numbers to show that given the growth imperatives of emerging economies such as India and China, a more feasible cut-off date for bringing down average per capita emissions to less than two tonnes, would be 2050 and not 2020. We can, he argues, work on capping the growth of carbon emissions, rather than negotiate on the basis of an absolute cap. This, in my view, has the kernel of a workable idea and our government will do well to look at this more carefully. In any case, being identified as principal naysayers earns us no brownie points from any constituency, and does not serve our national interests.

Section V

South Asia: India's Role

32

Take the Initiative

ENSURING a stable, peaceful and prosperous South Asia must be one of the highest policy priorities for India. Even our objective of reducing poverty will be better served if India adopted an even more active and coordinated South Asia policy because a large proportion of India's poorest, who live in the lagging border regions, are also prone to ethnic and extremist activities. Moreover, the fact that today China has a larger trade volume with all South Asian economies compared with India should give us something to seriously ponder about.

South Asia's intra-regional trade, which was 19 per cent of the region's total trade in 1950, has come down to a mere 5.6 per cent in 2007. A once deeply integrated and connected regional economy has been allowed to get increasingly fragmented and the investment climate for cross-border investment allowed to deteriorate to the point that there is hardly any capital flow at all across borders in South Asia except between India and Nepal and, now starting to increase, between Sri Lanka and India. The central question is what can India do to promote regional cooperation and make this process less vulnerable to random political and other shocks? The basic premise in answering this question must be that India has to be the lead player in promoting this regional cooperation and we cannot afford to take a stance that 'we can only try that much and no more.' The stakes are just too high. Deepening and broadening of economic ties amongst South Asian economies can be one of the most

effective tools against a further deterioration of political conditions and a powerful antidote against rising extremist tendencies of various shades in the region.

There are, however, still a few amongst the Indian policy influencing and policymaking circles who believe that India should simply stop wasting time and effort in promoting SAARC or the narrower agenda of economic cooperation as enshrined under South Asian Free Trade Area (SAFTA). This argument for giving SAARC a little more than lip service (keep the shop going without expecting it to ever make real progress!) has several well nuanced and seductive aspects. First, India is just too big for the region with about 80 per cent of the region's economic output and even an larger share in total regional population. The huge asymmetry does not lend itself to cooperation as the others will be in constant fear of the 'big brother' taking over. Second, India's legitimate global aspirations will be compromised if we get ensnared in thankless regional issues. Third, regional cooperation will be a bi-product of sustaining a high economic growth momentum in India as this will force our neighbours to recognise that India can in any case go alone and, moreover, give them greater incentive to cooperate and take advantage of a rapidly expanding Indian domestic market. Finally, that given our size and the leverage that it provides us, we are better off dealing with our neighbours bilaterally as a regional arrangement only weakens our position and may compromise our national interests *vis-à-vis* these countries.

In the present globalised world, any country, howsoever small, can successfully thwart bilateral pressure. Our past insistence on bilateralism only exacerbated the 'fear of the big brother' in our neighbours who justifiably resented and resisted this. It also encourages our neighbours to look for support and succour from China, which it of course accepts with thanks. This makes South Asia a more intensively contested space than warranted by the region's historical and geographic contiguity and the shared culture, language, religion and other social traits. Thankfully, Indian policy stance towards SAARC has shifted decisively from seeing it as an attempt by smaller neighbouring countries 'to gang up against us' to a more benevolent view that sees it as deepening and broadening economic flows in the region that will yield significant gains for us as well. This needs to be reinforced by more proactively facilitating regional and subregional infrastructure investments and improving trade facilitation and connectivity.

The issue of India's 'bigness' can be addressed to a large extent by India further reinforcing its stance of unilateral concessions and initiatives to reflect its cognisance of the existing asymmetry. The next steps, after having already offered duty and quota-free imports from our least developed neighbours, could be to unilaterally liberalise our visa regime with Pakistan and announce a substantial and unconditional grant right away for developing Nepal's hydro-electric potential. This will surely generate similar benefits to both partners as have accrued from projects in Bhutan and will be the best start for our relations with the newly constituted Republic of Nepal. India must now be seen as an active promoter of South Asian regional cooperation for it to be able to play its due role in the global arena.

33

New Beginnings

GIVEN the name and the reputation he carries, the Nepal Prime Minister's appearances and utterances in Delhi over the last two days were a study in contrast. He was mild, almost self-effacing, reportedly casual in his interactions and direct to the point. This is quite the exact opposite of most leaders from our other South Asian neighbours who can be ultra sensitive and often focus on scoring points rather than be focussed on the business at hand. This most positive and constructive trait of self-assurance and willingness to work as an equal partner, no doubt comes from being confident of the broad-based people's support at home, and a clear focus on the goal of raising the people's welfare and not on any personal agenda. Therefore, unlike in the past, personal egos and sensitivities, which have often been the bane of cross-border relations in South Asia are firmly in the background.

And the results are there for all of us to see. On offer are openings for exploiting the hydro power potential with Prachanda talking of up to 20,000 MW being available for harnessing by the two sides either by the private or public sector or in partnership. He also brought up the construction of the east-west railway corridor across the *terai*. This is an offer that India should seize with utmost alacrity. The project has the potential to transform the backward and lagging border regions of Northern Indian states. Their chief ministers, one of whom rightly made the trip to Delhi, should pursue this project with maximum energy and attention. Improving connectivity from the western reaches of Uttar

Pradesh *terai* to Bhutan and Sikkim borders will improve the security situation by opening up this region which is currently plagued by militancy and terrorist activity.

More important, the two sides have agreed to revisit the Indo-Nepal treaty of 1950. This has been a major irritant in our bilateral relations, especially for Nepal, which has seen it as an inequitable and unfair document. The Government of India's readiness to revise, upgrade and rethink the treaty reflects the changed stance in South Block *vis-à-vis* our neighbours. This welcome change did not go unnoticed by Prachanda who is reported to have remarked that his country, '...respects the new awareness in India for a stable and prosperous Nepal...'. On earlier occasions, India agreed to a review of the 58-year old treaty but with the rider that the review would also cover the clauses relating to the special relationship between the two countries. The crux of this special relationship is the free movement of Nepalese people into India. The Indian rider on this was naturally seen by Nepal as an implicit threat as the Nepalese still rely so heavily on employment and study opportunities in India. Hopefully, Nepal's economy will now pick up in tandem with the growth momentum in the Indian economy, because the new government is likely to be more honestly and seriously engaged in improving the lot of its common people than the monarchy could ever be. Nonetheless, I sincerely hope that the Indian side gives its commitment that we will never raise the special relationship provisions but, of course, be open to discussing it provided the Nepalese want to do so. This issue will never be raised by our side. There is simply no purpose in doing so because given our borders and the nature of the population on either side of the border, there will always be cross-border movement of people. The only real choice is whether to keep it legal or make it illegal and, thus even harder to monitor. There are countless examples across the world that fences and even oceans cannot hold back those who are determined to make a better life across national borders. Only the costs of doing so increases for all concerned.

It was most heartening to see that the *crème de la crème* of the capital's diplomatic, bureaucratic and security establishment was present at Prachanda's lecture at the India International Centre, Delhi. Curiosity brought along a few, but the majority came to listen to Prachanda's vision for a new Nepal and the future of Indo-Nepal relations. And they could not have been disappointed, though the lecture was unduly short and he could have done well to address security issues as they bother India, but Prachanda had discussed these with Indian officials anyway. To my very pleasant surprise, the large Nepalese delegation included businessmen and some of Indian origin as well. This is again a good sign showing that Nepal's Maoists are pragmatic to the core and will tailor their political and economic policy stance to suit ground realities rather than be slave to any ideology, as our leftists are wont to do. This characteristic has helped them get into power and become perhaps the only armed movement which could secure political power through the ballot box. Prachanda's visit to Rajnath Singh's residence and admission that Maoists have no issues with the Hindu faith, the practising faith of the large majority in Nepal, reflects the same pragmatic vein.

This visit should mark the beginning of a more constructive and positive phase in Indo-Nepal relations. The two sides can be truly equal partners in the shared journey of taking our people out of abject poverty.

Both countries are part of the same ecological, geographic and economic formation and a number of problems, including the management of Himalayan water resources, must be handled jointly. Our diplomacy, based on our newly adopted stance of asymmetrical reciprocity and strict equality in mutual relations must ensure that new Nepal finds enough reasons, rooted in its own clearly perceived national interests, to permit a southward tilt in its avowed policy of equidistance between its two large neighbours, the earlier visit to the Beijing Olympics notwithstanding.

34

Whose Side are we on?

SECURITY hawks, the media's foreign policy experts and the political class had a field day after July's Indo-Pakistani joint statement. Particularly for the Bhartiya Janta Party (BJP), whose astute leader Atal Bihari Vajpayee once took the boldest of steps to liberate India from its Pakistan obsession, nationalism seems confined to overtly displaying our superiority over a smaller neighbour, one fighting with its back to the wall against destabilising forces. Good foreign policy, however, has to be more nuanced so that our long-term national interests are served.

To better appreciate complex diplomatic endeavours, we must start by taking note of some facts. First, India accounts for about 80 per cent of South Asian GDP. Being so dominant, it has to bear an asymmetric responsibility for achieving stability, peace and prosperity in South Asia. This must be the bedrock of our neighbourhood policy. Second, we cannot choose our neighbours and should work with whoever we can to help Pakistan defeat the *jihadis*. Otherwise, there will be negative outcomes for our own experiment in building a pluralistic, multiethnic and democratic society. Third, the strategic balance between the two countries must surely rule out any ideas of a decisive military victory. That road leads only to mutually assured destruction. We may well have to bite the bullet one day, but it is best avoided. Fourth, there is not one monolithic Pakistan we can engage with. A choice must be made. There is the Pakistan of the armed forces which treats the country and its people as a fiefdom to be exploited for personal benefit. There is another Pakistan

toiling in poverty, deprivation and backwardness for which succour from daily injustices is welcome from any quarter. Fundamentalists, meanwhile, see themselves as guardians of the Pakistani state and true representatives of the Islamic republic. They see victory within their grasp because they have duped the army into believing that it can calibrate the growth of *jihadism*.

There is also the Pakistan of the rising middle class which wants modernisation but equates it with neither westernisation nor Islamisation. They are as horrified as we are at a video showing Taliban goons caning a woman and yet, like us, do not want to succumb entirely to the Coca-Cola culture. The *sufi* and *pir* traditions, to which prime minister Yousuf Raza Gilani and brave journalists, judges and lawyers belong, are also part of this Pakistan. The small, almost inconsequential section of westernised, 'liberated' men and women is yet another Pakistan. There is also the Pakistan of the *mohajirs* who see themselves as increasingly marginalised and resent that. Finally, there is the Pakistan whose political leaders represent growing popular aspirations for freedom and rule of law.

India must choose which Pakistan it wants to support, and which it wants to isolate and hopefully defeat over time. Clearly, we must work to erode the credibility and legitimacy of Pakistan's armed forces establishment, whose very reason to be is its festering animosity towards India. Islamic fundamentalists are the second group to be opposed. It is not mere coincidence that the two are aligned in vicious opposition to India and subvert by coordinated, violent means any move to improve bilateral relations. Pakistan-bashing, on which some sections of India's political spectrum and media thrive, strengthens the hands of these two groups. Nothing serves their purpose better than a bellicose India flexing its muscles and vocal cords against Pakistan. The reaction to Sharm-el-Sheikh must have been music to their ears.

The Pakistan to be supported is today most effectively represented by Gilani. He comes from a sufi family, is a thorough professional with well-established credentials for integrity. He is seen as distinct from his president who comes from a completely different background and perhaps with his own agenda. Gilani represents the aspirations, weaknesses and strengths of the Pakistani middle class which desires better and open relations with its counterparts across the Wagah border. Sharm-el-Sheikh was manifestly designed to support him and prevent him from relying completely on Rawalpindi, the *jihadis* or Asif Zardari for his political survival.

India must continue to make bold attempts to improve ties and strengthen Pakistan's elected leadership to give it the wherewithal to begin confronting religious fundamentalists and resisting the armed forces establishment, the two worst enemies of the Pakistani people. At Sharm-el-Sheikh, India gave away nothing in real terms. It only provided Gilani an opportunity to claim a breakthrough with his own hawks. If the strategy works, we would have an interlocutor with credibility and some capacity to resist the two groups most inimical to our interests.

What possible end can be served if Indo-Pak relations remain stalemated? Those who criticise initiatives to engage Pakistan should then suggest a more effective means of improving ties and collaborating with it to fight *jihadi* terrorists who, as agreed by the two countries earlier, are a menace for both.

Index

Sources

CHAPTER NO./TITLE/SOURCE

1. The many futures of India
   Live Mint, November 4, 2009.

2. The global crisis and India's growth rate
   Business Standard, December 3, 2008.

3. The global meltdown and Indian economic prospects
   Hindu, March 10, 2009.

4. The sky is not falling yet
   Business Standard, October 09, 2008.

5. Time to play it cool
   DNA, October 27, 2008.

6. Headed for a soft landing?
   Financial Chronicle, September 21, 2008.

7. A counter-inflation subsidy
   Live Mint, January 27, 2010.

8. Three critical reform priorities
   Financial Chronicle, May 14, 2009.

9. Time to consolidate reforms
   Financial Chronicle, December 25, 2008.

10. Focus on Follow-up
    Live Mint, January 13, 2010.

11. Reviving Manufacturing
    Live Mint, December 02, 2009.

12. Minimizing uncertainty
    Live Mint, December 16, 2009.

13. Lessons from Korea
    Live Mint, February 10, 2010.

14. Farm fresh from Argentina
    Live Mint, March 24, 2010.

15   Liberating the Farmer
     Live Mint, April 7, 2010.

16   Crying out for speedy reforms
     Financial Chronicle, October 22, 2009.

17   Big retail, big benefits
     Financial Chronicle, May 29, 2008.

18   Bold vision needed for exports
     Financial Chronicle, August 20, 2009.

19   The mother of all bailouts
     Financial Chronicle, October 2, 2008.

20   Protectionism and Obama
     Financial Chronicle, November 13, 2008.

21   How to beat the downturn
     Financial Chronicle, December 11, 2008.

22   Waiting for the Chinese switch
     Financial Chronicle, April 30, 2009

23   China's Investment story
     Live Mint, November 18, 2009

24   Challenges ahead for G20
     Financial Chronicle, April 2, 2009

25   Dragon conquers G20 summit
     Financial Chronicle, April 16, 2009

26   Contours of global governance
     Financial Chronicle, September 17, 2009.

27   Tangible results of Pittsburgh
     Financial Chronicle, October 1, 2009.

28   India & WTO: Rethink needed
     Business Standard, June 6, 2009.

29   Pumping new life into Doha round
     Financial Chronicle, September 3, 2009

30   Are we isolated on climate change?
     Financial Chronicle, August 6, 2009.

31   Take the initiative
     August 18, 2008.

32   New beginnings
     DNA, September 23, 2008.

33   Whose side are we on?
     Times of India, September 9, 2009.